365
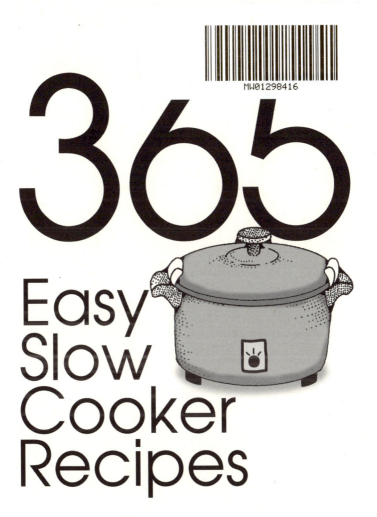
Easy
Slow
Cooker
Recipes

SWEETWATER
PRESS

365 Easy Slow Cooker Recipes

Copyright © 2008 by Cliff Road Books

Produced by arrangement with Sweetwater Press

All rights reserved. No part of this work may be reproduced or transmitted in any form or by any electronic or mechanical means, including information storage and retrieval systems, without written permission of the publisher.

The trademarked brand names used in some of the recipes of this book are integral to those recipes and do not represent endorsement by the brands or their owners.

While every effort has been made to ensure the accuracy of the recipes in this book, the publisher is not responsible for inaccuracies or less than satisfactory results. The publisher shall not be liable or responsible for any loss, injury, or damage allegedly arising from any information or suggestion in this book.

Printed in the United States of America

ISBN-13: 978-1-58173-730-1
ISBN-10: 1-58173-730-0

Design by Miles G. Parsons

365 Easy Slow Cooker Recipes

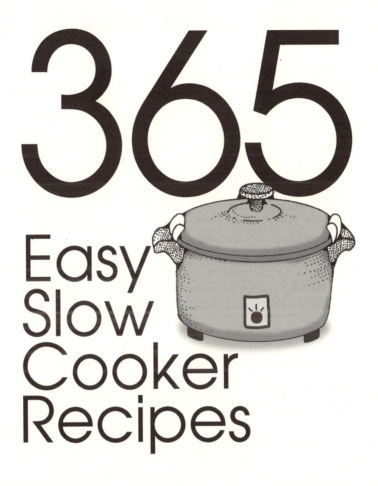

A Recipe for Every Day of the Year

Nicole Phillips

SWEETWATER
PRESS

Table of Contents

Introduction 7

Appetizers 9

Vegetables and Side Dishes 27

Soups and Stews 45

Beef, Lamb, and Pork 113

Poultry 155

Seafood 203

Desserts 221

Beverages 239

Index 244

INTRODUCTION

The value of a great, home-cooked meal can never be overestimated. Unfortunately, in these times of instant gratification, fast food and take-out too often replace home cooking. It seems that preparing a meal is just too much trouble for most people. *365 Easy Slow Cooker Recipes* was created with these folks in mind.

For those who like to make simple, inexpensive, yet delicious meals, *365 Easy Slow Cooker Recipes* is an indispensable resource. While the recipes in this volume were designed for the home cook's greatest ease, they are not lacking in taste or sophistication. The collection features unique dishes from around the globe, including Cantonese Pork, Lamb and Veggie Curry, Chicken Tacos, and dozens more. Classic American fare and comfort foods, such as Chicken Noodle Soup and Pork Roast, are incorporated as well. Gourmets will have no trouble finding recipes in this book to satisfy their highly developed palates, and novice chefs will be relieved by its simple instructions and quick preparation times.

With *365 Easy Slow Cooker Recipes*, great cooking can be enjoyed every night of the week with few ingredients and minimal effort. For delicious, straightforward, hassle-free recipes, you need not look further than this collection.

Nicole Phillips

APPETIZERS

Appetizer Ribs

3½ pounds spare ribs, cut into individual ribs
Salt and black pepper, to taste
2 cups water
Garlic salt, to taste
1 (8-ounce) bottle Russian salad dressing
1 (6-ounce) can pineapple juice

Season ribs with salt and pepper. Place in slow cooker and cover with water. Cover and cook on low 6 to 7 hours, or until meat is tender. Drain. Arrange ribs on broiler pan, and sprinkle with garlic salt. Combine salad dressing and pineapple juice, and brush top side of ribs with sauce. Broil until brown. Turn ribs and brush other side with sauce; broil until this side is also brown. Makes 8 servings.

Bacon Horseradish Dip

3 (8-ounce) packages cream cheese, cubed and softened
1 (12-ounce) package shredded Cheddar cheese
1 cup half-and-half
⅓ cup chopped green onion
3 garlic cloves, minced
3 tablespoon prepared horseradish
1 tablespoon Worcestershire sauce
½ teaspoon black pepper
12 slices bacon, crisply cooked and crumbled
Corn chips or assorted crackers

Combine all ingredients except bacon and chips or crackers in a slow cooker. Cover and cook on low for 4 to 5 hours or on high for 2 to 2½ hours, stirring once halfway through. Stir in bacon. Eat cooled or at room temperature. Serve with corn chips, potato chips, or crackers. Makes 8 servings.

Bacon Onion Dip

1 (8-ounce) package light cream cheese, softened
1 cup light sour cream
½ cup Cheddar cheese, shredded
2 green onions, finely chopped
6 slices bacon, finely chopped and cooked
Potato chips or crackers

Place cream cheese, sour cream, Cheddar cheese, and green onions in a slow cooker. Crumble the bacon and sprinkle on top. Cover and cook on high for 1 hour or until cheese is melted. Do not stir. Reduce heat to low until ready to serve. Makes 12 servings.

Beef Dip

1 pound ground beef
1 cup chopped onion
½ cup chopped green bell pepper
2 garlic cloves, minced
3 cups grated Monterey Jack cheese
½ cup chopped chile pepper
2 teaspoons Worcestershire sauce
1 cup tomato sauce
½ teaspoon chili powder
Tortilla chips

In a large nonstick skillet, combine beef, onion, bell pepper, and garlic. Cook over medium heat until beef is browned. Pour into a slow cooker, and add the cheese, chile pepper, Worcestershire sauce, tomato sauce, and chili powder. Stir well, cover, and cook on low for 2 hours. Serve with tortilla chips. Makes 12 servings.

Boiled Peanuts

2 pounds fresh peanuts, uncooked and in shells
½ cup salt

Fill a slow cooker with peanuts. Cover with water and add salt; stir. Cover and cook on low for 12 to 18 hours, or until peanuts are soft. Drain and serve. Makes 12 servings.

Cajun Pecans

1 pound pecan halves
¼ cup melted butter
1 tablespoon chili powder
1 teaspoon salt
1 teaspoon dried basil
1 teaspoon dried oregano
1 teaspoon dried thyme
½ teaspoon onion powder
¼ teaspoon garlic powder
¼ teaspoon cayenne pepper

Combine all ingredients in slow cooker. Cover and cook on high for 15 minutes. Turn to low and continue to cook uncovered for 2 hours, stirring occasionally. Transfer nuts to a baking sheet and cool completely. Makes 12 servings.

Cheddar Potato Slices

1 (10¾-ounce) can cream of mushroom soup
½ teaspoon paprika
½ teaspoon black pepper
4 medium baking potatoes, sliced ¼-inch thick
1 cup shredded Cheddar cheese

Combine soup, paprika, and pepper. Arrange potatoes in bottom of lightly greased slow cooker. Sprinkle with cheese. Spoon soup mixture over cheese. Cover and cook on high 3 to 4 hours, until potatoes are tender. Keep on low until serving. Makes 8 servings.

Cheesy Chile and Refried Bean Dip

2 (16-ounce) cans refried beans
2 (8-ounce) packages cream cheese, cubed
2 onions, chopped
2 (4-ounce) cans diced green chiles, drained
2 cups shredded Cheddar cheese, divided
Tortilla chips

In a slow cooker, combine beans, cream cheese, onion, and chiles. Cover and cook for 2 to 3 hours until hot, stirring twice during cooking. Mix in ½ cup cheese. Sprinkle remaining cheese on top and serve with tortilla chips. Makes 12 servings.

Cheesy New Orleans Shrimp Dip

1 slice bacon
3 medium onions, chopped
1 garlic clove, minced
4 jumbo shrimp, peeled and deveined
1 medium tomato, peeled and chopped
3 cups shredded Monterey Jack cheese
4 drops hot pepper sauce
⅛ teaspoon cayenne pepper
Dash black pepper
Tortilla chips

Cook bacon until crisp, drain on paper towel, and crumble. Sauté onion and garlic in bacon drippings and drain on paper towel. Coarsely chop shrimp. Combine all ingredients except chips in slow cooker. Cover and cook on low 1 hour, or until cheese is melted. Thin with milk if too thick. Serve with chips. Makes 6 to 8 servings.

Chili con Queso

1 (16-ounce) jar Mexican or plain pasteurized processed cheese spread
1⅓ cups chunky salsa
1 (4-ounce) can diced green chiles, drained
¼ teaspoon black pepper

Combine all ingredients in a slow cooker. Cover and cook on low for 2 to 2½ hours, or until cheese is melted, stirring twice during cooking. Remove the lid from the slow cooker, and cook on high for 1 hour longer, until mixture is hot. Makes 8 servings.

Chili Dip

1 pound ground beef, cooked
2 (16-ounce) cans refried beans
1 large bottle picante sauce
1 medium onion, chopped
1 pint sour cream
1 cup shredded Cheddar cheese
½ teaspoon chili powder
Salt and black pepper, to taste
Seeded and chopped jalapeños, to taste

Combine all ingredients in a slow cooker, and cook for 4 to 6 hours on low. Serve with raw vegetables or chips. Makes 12 servings.

Chili Nuts

¼ cup melted butter
2 (12-ounce) cans cocktail peanuts
1 tablespoon chili seasoning

Pour butter over nuts in slow cooker. Sprinkle in dry chili mix. Toss together. Cover. Heat on low for 2 to 2½ hours. Turn to high. Remove lid and cook for 10 or 15 minutes. Serve warm or cool. Makes 12 servings.

Cocktail Sausages

¾ cup apricot preserves
¼ cup prepared yellow mustard
2 scallions, chopped
½ pound precooked mini smoked sausages

Combine all ingredients in a slow cooker. Cover and cook on low for 4 hours. Makes 4 servings.

Crab Dip

2 (8-ounce) packages cream cheese, cubed and softened
2 (6½-ounce) cans crabmeat, drained
¼ cup sliced green onions
¼ cup sour cream
2 teaspoons Worcestershire sauce
Crackers

Combine all ingredients except crackers in a slow cooker. Cover and cook on high until cheese melts, about 30 minutes. Stir well. Serve with crackers. Makes 8 servings.

Cranberry Turkey Balls

2 large eggs, well beaten
2 pounds ground turkey
1 cup dry breadcrumbs
2 tablespoons minced sweet onion
2 garlic cloves, minced
⅓ cup minced fresh parsley
⅓ cup ketchup
2 tablespoons soy sauce
½ teaspoon salt
¼ teaspoon black pepper
1 (16-ounce) can whole-berry cranberry sauce
1½ cups chili sauce
1 tablespoon brown sugar
1 tablespoon prepared mustard
1 tablespoon freshly squeezed lemon juice
2 garlic cloves, minced

Combine eggs, turkey, breadcrumbs, onion, garlic, parsley, ketchup, soy sauce, salt, and pepper. Form into 1-inch balls. Place balls on an ungreased baking sheet with 1-inch sides. Bake uncovered at 450° for 8 to 10 minutes, or until turkey is no longer pink. Drain as necessary.

Meanwhile, in a slow cooker, mix together cranberry sauce, chili sauce, brown sugar, mustard, lemon juice, and garlic. Stir well over low setting. Add cooked turkey balls to cranberry mixture in slow cooker. Stir well to coat with sauce. Cover and cook on low for 2 hours, stirring occasionally. Serve warm. Makes 12 servings.

This recipe used by permission of the National Turkey Federation.

Enchilada Dip

2 pounds boneless, skinless chicken thighs
1 (10-ounce) can enchilada sauce
2 (8-ounce) packages cream cheese, cubed and softened
4 cups shredded pepper Jack cheese

Combine chicken and enchilada sauce in a slow cooker. Cover and cook on low for 8 to 10 hours, or until chicken is thoroughly cooked. Using two forks, shred chicken in the sauce.

Stir cream cheese and Jack cheese in the slow cooker; mix well. Cover and cook on low for 30 minutes, stirring twice, until mixture is blended and cheese is melted. Makes 12 servings.

Hearty Broccoli Dip

1 pound ground beef
1 pound processed American cheese, cubed
1 (10¾-ounce) can condensed cream of mushroom soup, undiluted
1 (10-ounce) package frozen chopped broccoli, thawed and drained
2 tablespoons salsa
Tortilla chips

In a large skillet, cook beef over medium heat until no longer pink; drain. Transfer to a slow cooker. Add cheese, soup, broccoli, and salsa; mix well. Cover and cook on low for 2 to 3 hours or until heated through, stirring after 1 hour. Serve with tortilla chips. Makes 12 servings.

365 Easy Slow Cooker Recipes

Hot Spinach Cheese Dip

1 (16- to 20-ounce) package frozen chopped spinach, thawed and squeezed dry
2 (8-ounce) packages cream cheese, cubed and softened
¾ cup chopped green onion
½ teaspoon garlic powder
¼ teaspoon coarsely ground black pepper
¼ teaspoon paprika
2 cups shredded Cheddar cheese, divided
1 (8-ounce) can water chestnuts, drained and chopped
Assorted crackers, chips, or vegetable dippers

In slow cooker, combine spinach and cream cheese. Add green onions, garlic powder, pepper, and paprika. Cover and cook for 2 hours until very hot, stirring once or twice. Reserve ¼ cup of shredded cheese for topping. Stir in the remaining cheese and chopped water chestnuts. Sprinkle reserved cheese over top. Serve with chips, crackers, or vegetables for dipping. Makes 8 servings.

Kielbasa Sausage

2 (16-ounce) packages kielbasa sausage, cut into 1-inch pieces
2 cups grape jelly
2 cups ketchup

In a large skillet, brown the sausage over medium-high heat. Meanwhile, combine jelly and ketchup in a slow cooker. Cook on medium until combined, stirring occasionally. Add kielbasa and reduce heat to low. Cover and cook for 1 hour. Makes 8 servings.

Marinara Dip

4 (14-ounce) cans diced tomatoes with Italian seasoning, undrained
2 onions, chopped
8 garlic cloves, minced
1 (6-ounce) can tomato paste
½ cup water
2 teaspoons dried Italian seasoning

Combine all ingredients in a slow cooker, cover, and cook on low for 8 to 10 hours. Serve over pasta or as a dip for garlic bread, bread sticks, or cheese sticks. Makes 12 servings.

Marinated Mushrooms

2 cups soy sauce
2 cups water
1 cup butter
2 cups white sugar
4 (8-ounce) packages fresh mushrooms, stems removed

In a medium saucepan over low heat, mix soy sauce, water, and butter. Stir until the butter has melted, and then gradually mix in the sugar until it is completely dissolved. Place mushrooms in a slow cooker set to low, and cover with the soy sauce mixture. Cook for 8 to 10 hours, stirring approximately every hour. Chill before serving. Makes 12 servings.

Party Snack Mix

3 cups thin pretzel sticks
2 cups wheat cereal
2 cups rice cereal
3 cups mixed nuts
½ cup butter, melted
¼ cup Worcestershire sauce
2 tablespoons grated Parmesan cheese
1 teaspoon seasoned salt
1 teaspoon garlic salt

In a slow cooker, combine the pretzels, cereals, and nuts. In a bowl, combine the remaining ingredients and stir well. Pour into slow cooker and toss to coat. Cook uncovered for 2 hours, stirring frequently. Reduce heat to low, and cook for another 2 hours. Makes 12 servings.

Reuben Spread

½ pound corned beef, shredded or chopped
1 (16-ounce) can sauerkraut, well drained
1 to 2 cups shredded Swiss cheese
1 to 2 cups shredded Cheddar cheese
1 cup mayonnaise
Snack rye bread
Thousand Island dressing (optional)

Combine all ingredients except bread and Thousand Island dressing in slow cooker and mix well. Cover and cook on high for 1 to 2 hours until heated through, stirring occasionally. Turn to low and keep warm in cooker while serving. Put spread on bread slices, and top individual servings with Thousand Island dressing, if desired. Makes 5 cups.

Roasted Pepper and Artichoke Spread

1 cup grated Parmesan cheese
½ cup mayonnaise
1 (8-ounce) package cream cheese, softened
1 garlic clove, minced
1 (14-ounce) can artichoke hearts, drained and finely chopped
⅓ cup finely chopped roasted red bell pepper
Crackers or vegetables

Combine Parmesan cheese, mayonnaise, cream cheese, and garlic in food processor. Process until smooth. Place mixture in slow cooker. Add artichoke hearts and red bell pepper. Stir well, cover, and cook on low 1 hour. Stir again. Serve with crackers or vegetables. Makes 3 cups.

Salsa

12 small tomatoes, cored and chopped
3 garlic cloves, minced
1 onion, chopped
2 jalapeños, seeded and chopped
½ cup chopped cilantro
¾ teaspoon salt
Tortilla chips

In a slow cooker, combine the tomatoes, garlic, onion, and jalapeños. Cover and cook on high for 2½ hours, or until tomatoes are soft. Remove from heat and let cool. Spoon the mixture into a food processor or blender. Add the cilantro and salt; blend until smooth. Serve with tortilla chips. Makes 8 servings.

Seafood Fondue

2 (10¾-ounce) cans cream of celery soup
2 cups grated sharp Cheddar cheese
1 cup cooked and chopped crabmeat
½ to 1 cup cooked and diced lobster
½ cup cooked and chopped shrimp
Dash paprika
Dash ground nutmeg
Dash cayenne pepper
1 loaf of crusty bread, cut into 1-inch cubes

Butter bottom and sides of slow cooker. Combine all ingredients except bread cubes in prepared slow cooker; stir well. Cover and cook on low for about 2 hours, or until cheese is melted. Keep slow cooker on low for serving. Serve with bread cubes for dipping. Makes 6 to 7 cups

Sloppy Joe Dip

2 pounds lean ground beef
1 onion, chopped
¼ cup water
½ teaspoon salt
¼ teaspoon black pepper
1 (12-ounce) bottle chili sauce or ketchup
Tortilla chips

Cook ground beef in a heavy skillet until brown and crumbly. Drain thoroughly and place in slow cooker. Add onion, water, salt, pepper, and chili sauce or ketchup. Mix well. Cover slow cooker and cook on low for 4 to 6 hours, until onions are tender. Serve with tortilla chips. Makes 12 servings.

Spicy Beef Dip

2 pounds lean ground beef
1 onion, chopped
1 (10¾-ounce) can cream of mushroom soup
1 pound processed cheese, cubed
1 (12-ounce) jar sliced jalapeño, drained

Place lean ground beef and onion in a large, deep skillet over medium high heat. Cook until beef is evenly brown and onion is soft. Drain and turn heat to medium low. Mix in soup, processed cheese, and jalapeño. Cook and stir until all ingredients are well blended, about 10 minutes. Transfer the mixture to a medium bowl. Cover and chill in the refrigerator 8 hours, or overnight. Reheat the mixture in a slow cooker, mixing in about 1 tablespoon of water to thin if necessary. Makes 12 servings.

Spicy Chicken Wings

2 cups brown sugar
¼ cup hot sauce
½ cup butter
4 tablespoons soy sauce
4 pounds chicken wings

In a saucepan, combine the brown sugar, hot sauce, butter, and soy sauce. Heat until butter is melted. Put the chicken wings in a slow cooker, and pour sauce over top. Cover and cook on low for 4 to 5 hours. Makes 12 servings.

Spinach and Artichoke Dip

1 (14-ounce) can artichoke hearts, drained and chopped
1 cup chopped spinach
1 cup shredded mozzarella cheese
1 (8-ounce) package cream cheese, cubed
½ cup grated Parmesan cheese
1 teaspoon garlic powder
¼ teaspoon black pepper
½ cup chopped red bell pepper
Tortilla chips

Combine all ingredients in a slow cooker. Cover and cook on high for 2 hours, or until cheeses are melted. Serve with tortilla chips. Makes 12 servings.

Stuffed Chicken Rolls

6 boneless, skinless chicken breasts
6 slices fully cooked ham
6 slices Swiss cheese
¼ cup all purpose flour
¼ cup grated Parmesan cheese
½ teaspoon rubbed sage
¼ teaspoon paprika
¼ teaspoon black pepper
¼ cup vegetable oil
1 (10¾-ounce) can cream of chicken soup
½ cup chicken broth
Fresh parsley

Flatten chicken to ⅛-inch thickness. Place ham and cheese on breast and roll it up; tuck and secure with toothpicks. Combine flour, Parmesan, sage, paprika, and pepper. Coat chicken, cover, and refrigerate for 1 hour. In large skillet, brown chicken rolls in oil over medium heat. Transfer to slow cooker with combined soup and broth. Cover and cook for 4 to 5 hours. Makes 6 servings.

365 Easy Slow Cooker Recipes

Sweet and Sour Meatballs

2 pounds precooked frozen meatballs
1 cup grape jelly
2 cups cocktail sauce

Heat meatballs in oven as directed on package. Place in a slow cooker. Mix jelly and cocktail sauce thoroughly, pour over meatballs and stir well. Cover and cook on high 1 to 2 hours, until sauce is hot. Turn heat to low until ready to serve, stirring occasionally. Makes 8 servings.

Turkey and Cheese Dip

1¼ pounds ground turkey
1¼ pounds hot Italian turkey sausage, casings removed
1 (12-ounce) can sliced jalapeño, drained
1 medium onion, finely chopped
1 pound processed cheese, cubed
½ pound Cheddar cheese, cubed
1 (8-ounce) package cream cheese, cubed
1 cup cottage cheese
1 cup sour cream
1 (15-ounce) can diced tomatoes, drained
3 garlic cloves, minced
Salt and black pepper, to taste
Crisp crackers and tortilla chips

In a large skillet over medium heat, cook and stir ground turkey and sausage until cooked through. Drain and transfer to a large slow cooker. Add jalapeño, onion, cheeses, sour cream, tomatoes, garlic, and seasonings. Stir and cook covered for 1½ to 2 hours until cheeses are melted. Serve with crackers and tortilla chips. Makes 12 servings.

This recipe used by permission of the National Turkey Federation.

VEGETABLES AND SIDE DISHES

365 Easy Slow Cooker Recipes

⭐ Baked Beans

½ pound ground beef, cooked and drained
1 (16-ounce) can red kidney beans, drained
1 (16-ounce) can butter beans, drained
1 (16-ounce) can pork and beans *with honey*
1 small onion, chopped
¼ cup brown sugar
¼ cup ketchup
~~¼ cup barbecue sauce~~
2 tablespoons prepared mustard
~~2 tablespoons molasses~~
1 teaspoon salt *if needed*
½ teaspoon chili powder
¼ teaspoon black pepper

Combine all ingredients in a slow cooker. Cover and cook on low for 6 to 8 hours. Makes 6 to 8 servings.

Barbecued Pinto Beans

1 pound dried pinto beans
3 cups water
1 onion, chopped
1 (18-ounce) bottle barbecue sauce
¼ cup molasses
¼ teaspoon black pepper

Sort beans, rinse, and drain. Combine all ingredients in a slow cooker. Cover and cook on low for 8 to 9 hours, or until beans are tender. Makes 6 to 8 servings.

Caramelized Onions

6 large onions
2 tablespoons olive oil

Peel the onions and cut them into ¼-inch slices. Place the onions in the slow cooker, and sprinkle with oil. Cover and cook 8 to 10 hours, until the onions caramelize. Makes 3 cups.

Cheesy Asparagus

1 pound fresh asparagus
1½ tablespoons all-purpose flour
¼ teaspoon salt
Black pepper, to taste
¾ cup evaporated skim milk
1 cup grated sharp Cheddar cheese

Wash and trim asparagus (asparagus breaks naturally at the tough part of the stalk). Lay the spears in a slow cooker. Stir flour, salt, and pepper together in saucepan. Whisk in evaporated skim milk gradually, until no lumps remain. Heat and stir until boiling and thickened. Stir in cheese to melt. Pour over asparagus. Cover and cook on low. Check for doneness at 2 hours if you like it crisp. Let it cook an hour longer if you like it softer. Makes 6 servings.

Cheesy Broccoli and Cauliflower

1 (10-ounce) package frozen broccoli
1 (10-ounce) package frozen cauliflower
Salt and black pepper, to taste
1 (10¾-ounce) can nacho cheese soup
4 slices bacon, cooked and crumbled

Place broccoli and cauliflower in a slow cooker. Season with salt and pepper to taste. Spoon soup over top. Sprinkle with bacon. Cover and cook on low for 4 to 6 hours. Makes 4 to 6 servings.

Cheesy Potatoes

1 (10¾-ounce) can condensed cream of mushroom soup
1 (8-ounce) container sour cream
1½ cups shredded Cheddar cheese
1 (32-ounce) package frozen hash brown potatoes

Coat slow cooker with cooking spray. Combine soup, sour cream, and cheese in medium bowl; mix well. Pour half of potatoes into the prepared slow cooker. Top with half of the sour cream mixture. Top with rest of potatoes and then remaining sour cream mixture, spreading evenly. Cover and cook on high for 3½ to 4½ hours. Makes 4 servings.

Cheesy Spinach

2 (10-ounce) packages frozen chopped spinach, thawed and well drained
2 cups small-curd cottage cheese
1½ cups shredded Cheddar cheese
3 eggs, lightly beaten
¼ cup margarine, cubed
¼ cup all-purpose flour
1 teaspoon salt

Combine all the ingredients in a large bowl. Pour into a greased slow cooker. Cover and cook on high for 1 hour. Reduce to low and cook 4 to 5 hours longer, or until a knife inserted comes out clean. Makes 6 to 8 servings.

Cinnamon Applesauce

10 large apples, peeled, cored, and chopped
1 cup sugar
½ cup water
1 teaspoon ground cinnamon
½ teaspoon ground nutmeg

Combine all ingredients in a slow cooker. Cover and cook on low for 8 to 10 hours. Makes 10 to 12 servings.

Collard Greens in Tomato Sauce

2 slices bacon
2 onions, finely chopped
2 garlic cloves, minced
1 teaspoon salt
½ teaspoon black pepper
2 cups tomatoes including juice, coarsely chopped
2 pounds fresh collard greens, tough stems removed and chopped into 2-inch lengths
Hot pepper sauce
Red vinegar

In skillet, cook bacon over medium heat until crisp. Drain on paper towel and crumble. Set aside. Drain all but 1 tablespoon fat from pan, and reduce heat to medium. Add onions to pan and cook, stirring, until softened. Add garlic, salt, and pepper, and cook, stirring, for 1 minute. Add tomatoes and bring to a boil.

Place greens in slow cooker. Add tomato mixture and stir to combine. Cover and cook on low for 6 hours or on high for 3 hours, until greens are tender. Serve with hot pepper sauce or a splash of vinegar, if desired. Top with crisp bacon. Makes 6 to 8 servings.

Fresh Veggie Lasagna

1½ cups shredded mozzarella cheese
½ cup part-skim ricotta cheese
⅓ cup grated Parmesan cheese
1 egg, lightly beaten
1 teaspoon dried oregano
¼ teaspoon garlic powder
1 cup low-sodium, fat-free marinara sauce (plus additional for serving)
1 medium zucchini, diced
4 no-boil lasagna noodles
1 (9-ounce) bag fresh baby spinach
1 cup thinly sliced mushrooms
Fresh basil leaves (optional)

Coat inside of slow cooker with nonstick cooking spray; set aside. In a small bowl, mix together mozzarella, ricotta, Parmesan, egg, oregano, and garlic powder.

Spread 2 tablespoons of marinara sauce in bottom of pot. Sprinkle half of the zucchini over sauce and top with one-third of cheese mixture. Break two noodles into pieces to cover cheese. Spread 2 tablespoons of sauce, and then layer half of the spinach and half of the mushrooms. Repeat layering, ending with cheese and remaining sauce. Firmly press ingredients into pot.

Cover and cook over low heat for 4 to 5 hours. Allow lasagna to rest 20 minutes before cutting into wedges to serve. Spoon a little extra sauce over each serving and top with a basil leaf, if desired. Makes 4 servings.

Gingered Carrots

12 carrots, peeled and sliced
⅓ cup Dijon mustard
½ cup brown sugar
1 teaspoon minced fresh ginger
½ teaspoon salt
⅛ teaspoon black pepper

Combine all ingredients in a slow cooker. Cover and cook on high for 2 to 3 hours or until carrots are tender, stirring twice during cooking. Makes 4 to 6 servings.

Glazed Carrots

2 pounds baby carrots
1½ cups water
¼ cup honey
2 tablespoons butter
¼ teaspoon salt
⅛ teaspoon black pepper

Combine carrots and water in a slow cooker. Cover and cook on low for 6 to 8 hours, or until carrots are tender when pierced with a fork. Drain carrots and return to slow cooker. Stir in honey, butter, salt, and pepper and mix well. Cover and cook on low 30 minutes until glazed. Makes 8 servings.

Harvest Potatoes

1 cup chicken broth
2 teaspoons pickling spice, tied in cheesecloth
4 large potatoes, peeled and cut into ¾-inch cubes
2 garlic cloves, pressed
Snipped fresh chives, for garnish (optional)

Pour the broth into a slow cooker, and place the spices in the center bottom of the cooker. Add the potatoes and garlic. Cover and cook on low for 5 to 6 hours. Garnish with chives. Makes 6 to 8 servings.

Home-Style Baked Beans

2½ cups dried beans
1 small onion, chopped
1 (2-ounce) piece salt pork
6 tablespoons ketchup
6 tablespoons molasses
¼ cup brown sugar
1 tablespoon dry mustard
1½ teaspoons salt
½ teaspoon black pepper

Soak beans overnight in water. The next day, boil beans for 1 hour. Transfer to a slow cooker and add all other ingredients. Cook on high for 3 hours, or on low for 10 to 12 hours. Add water as needed. Makes 8 servings.

Hot Dog Beans

1 package hot dogs, sliced
2 (16-ounce) cans baked beans
⅓ cup ketchup or barbecue sauce
¼ cup dark brown sugar
1½ tablespoons yellow mustard
½ teaspoon onion powder

Mix all ingredients together in a slow cooker. Cook for 1½ to 2½ hours on high or 4 to 8 hours on low. Makes 8 servings.

Hot German Potato Salad

6 cups sliced potatoes
1 cup chopped onion
1 cup chopped celery
½ cup water
¼ cup cider vinegar
2 tablespoons quick-cooking tapioca
1 tablespoon sugar
2 teaspoons dried parsley flakes
¼ teaspoon black pepper
¼ cup bacon bits

In a large bowl, combine potatoes, onion, and celery. Mix remaining ingredients except bacon in a small bowl; pour over potatoes, mixing well. Pour into slow cooker. Cover and cook on low for 8 to 10 hours, until potatoes are done. Stir in bacon bits. Makes 8 servings.

Lightened Mashed Potatoes

5 pounds Yukon gold potatoes, peeled and quartered
3 to 4 garlic cloves, peeled
2 (3-ounce) packages light cream cheese, softened
½ cup reduced-fat sour cream
½ cup nonfat plain yogurt
¼ cup egg substitute
2 teaspoons onion powder
1 teaspoon salt
½ teaspoon black pepper
1 tablespoon butter or margarine

Boil potatoes and garlic cloves until potatoes are tender; drain. Mash potatoes and garlic until there are no lumps. Add remaining ingredients except butter. Cook in slow cooker on low for 2 to 2½ hours or until heated through. Stir in butter before servings. Makes 12 servings.

Macaroni and Cheese

1 (16-ounce) box elbow macaroni
2 (12-ounce) cans evaporated milk
3 cups milk
3 cups grated sharp cheese
½ cup margarine
1 tablespoon minced onion
1 tablespoon oil
1 teaspoon salt
Black pepper, to taste

Put all the ingredients into a slow cooker. Cook on low for 3 to 4 hours until soft. Makes 4 servings.

Magnificent Mushrooms

1 pound mushrooms, sliced or whole
½ cup butter, cubed
1 tablespoon marjoram
1 teaspoon chives, minced
Salt and black pepper, to taste
¾ cup chicken broth

Place mushrooms in a slow cooker. Place butter on top. Mix remaining ingredients and pour over the top. Cover and cook on low for 4 to 6 hours. Makes 4 servings.

Mashed Potatoes

5 pounds potatoes, peeled and quartered
1 (8-ounce) package light cream cheese
1 cup light sour cream
2 teaspoons onion powder
1 teaspoon salt
½ teaspoon black pepper
2 egg whites, slightly beaten
1 tablespoon margarine

Cook the potatoes in a large pot of boiling water until they are tender, about 20 minutes. Drain; mash until there are no lumps. Add the cream cheese, sour cream, onion powder, salt, pepper, and egg whites; blend well. Spray a casserole with nonstick cooking spray. Add potato mixture. Dot with margarine. Cool slightly, cover, and refrigerate up to 7 days. Take potatoes out of refrigerator about 3½ hours before you plan to serve them. Place in a slow cooker. Dot with margarine or butter. Cook on low heat for 3 hours, stirring once or twice. Makes 12 servings.

Mixed Rice Pilaf

¾ cup wild rice
½ cup long grain brown rice
½ pound portobello mushrooms
1 (10¾-ounce) can cream of mushroom soup with roasted garlic
1½ cups water
⅛ teaspoon black pepper

Rinse rice and drain. Wipe mushrooms with a damp cloth, remove stems, and cut into 1-inch slices. Combine all ingredients in a slow cooker. Cover and cook on low for 6 to 7 hours, or until rice and mushrooms are tender. Makes 4 servings.

Peachy Sweet Potatoes

2 pounds sweet potatoes
1 cup peach pie filling
2 tablespoons butter, melted
¼ teaspoon salt
¼ teaspoon black pepper

Spray a slow cooker with nonstick cooking spray, and place sweet potatoes in the slow cooker. Add pie filling, melted butter, salt, and pepper, and mix well. Cover and cook on high for 2½ to 3½ hours, until potatoes are tender when pierced with a fork. Makes 4 servings.

Rice Pilaf

2 (14-ounce) cans chicken broth with roasted garlic
1⅔ cups water
3 cups long-grain white rice
½ cup minced onion
¼ teaspoon black pepper

Combine broth and water in a large bowl, and microwave on high until very hot, about 5 minutes. Spray a slow cooker with cooking spray. Combine rice, onion, and pepper in slow cooker, and mix to combine. Pour hot broth mixture over, and cover slow cooker. Cook on high for 1½ to 2 hours, until rice is tender. Stir and serve. Makes 8 servings.

Salt-Baked Potatoes

4 baking potatoes
Olive oil
Kosher salt

Scrub potatoes well, dry thoroughly with paper towels, prick with fork, and rub with olive oil. Put about an inch depth of salt into a slow cooker, lay potatoes on salt, and pour salt over top, so the potatoes are evenly covered. Cover and cook on high for about 2 hours, until potatoes are tender. Break through the salt crust, and lift out the potatoes, brushing gently to remove any salt. Makes 4 servings.

Southern Potatoes

2 pounds frozen hash browns
1 (10¾-ounce) can cream of mushroom soup
½ cup butter, melted
2 cups French onion dip

Mix together hash browns, soup, and butter, and put into a slow cooker. Cook on low for 6 to 8 hours. Add French onion dip 30 minutes before serving. Makes 6 to 8 servings.

Spaghetti Squash Frittatas

1 cup spaghetti squash, cooked and separated into strands
4 eggs, lightly beaten
2 tablespoons Italian parsley, chopped
3 tablespoons grated Parmesan cheese
1 cup red onion, finely chopped
3 to 4 garlic cloves, minced
½ teaspoon salt
½ teaspoon black pepper
⅛ teaspoon cayenne
1 tablespoon butter

Combine all ingredients in a large mixing bowl. Melt butter in a large skillet. Pour mixture into the skillet, and cook on low for about 12 to 15 minutes. Transfer to broiler for 2 to 3 minutes, or until top is browned. Makes 6 servings.

Vegetarian Enchilada Casserole

2 (16-ounce) cans black beans, rinsed and drained
1 pound corn kernels, thawed if frozen
3⅓ cups canned crushed tomatoes
1⅔ cups chunky style prepared salsa
1 (6-ounce) can tomato paste
1 (4-ounce) canned diced mild green chiles, drained
1½ tablespoons ground cumin
½ teaspoon garlic powder
6 corn tortillas
¼ cup olive slices, drained

Combine first eight ingredients in a bowl. Mix thoroughly. Pour about 1 cup of mixture into the bottom of a slow cooker on low heat. Spread evenly and top with 3 tortillas, cutting to fit pot. Spread ⅓ of remaining tomato mixture over top. Repeat layering process, ending with tomato mixture. Spread top evenly. Sprinkle with olives. Cover and cook on low heat about 5 hours. Serve hot. Makes 8 servings.

Vegetarian Stuffed Peppers

2 large green bell peppers
2 large red bell peppers
½ cup cooked white rice
1 (15-ounce) can whole kernel corn, drained
1 (2-ounce) can sliced olives, drained
3 green onions, chopped
¼ teaspoon seasoned salt
¼ teaspoon garlic pepper
1 (14½-ounce) can diced tomatoes, undrained, divided
⅓ cup vegetable broth
1 (6-ounce) can tomato paste

Slice tops off peppers and carefully remove seeds and inner ribs. Remove stems from tops and chop remaining pepper pieces. Stand the peppers upright in a slow cooker. In a medium bowl, combine chopped pepper tops, rice, corn, olives, green onions, seasoned salt, garlic pepper, and ¼ cup tomatoes. Mix well. Stuff peppers with corn mixture, dividing evenly and packing lightly. Mix remaining tomatoes and their liquid with broth and tomato paste until well blended. Pour over and around the peppers in slow cooker. Cover and cook on low for 6 to 7 hours, or until rice is cooked and peppers are tender but still hold their shape. Makes 4 servings.

Wild Rice

1½ cups long-grain brown or white rice
½ cup wild rice
1 (8-ounce) can mushrooms, sliced
4 cups water
1 bunch green onions, sliced
1 (1-ounce) envelope onion soup mix
1 tablespoon dried parsley

Combine all ingredients into a lightly greased slow cooker. Cook 2 to 2½ hours on high. Stir occasionally, especially near end of cooking. Makes 4 servings.

SOUPS AND STEWS

8-Can Soup

1 pound ground beef
1 (16-ounce) can chili with beans
1 (16-ounce) can chili without beans
1 (14½-ounce) can tomatoes with green chiles
1 (14½-ounce) can diced tomatoes
1 (11-ounce) can whole corn
1 (11-ounce) can mixed vegetables
1 (10¾-ounce) can condensed tomato soup
1 (10¾-ounce) can condensed vegetable soup

Brown ground beef and drain. Put into large slow cooker. Add contents of all cans to slow cooker with their juices. Cook on low until thoroughly heated. Makes 8 to 10 servings.

6-Can Chili

½ cup barbecue sauce
1 (28-ounce) can chopped tomatoes with juice
2 (15-ounce) cans chili without beans
1 (15½-ounce) can pinto or dark or light red kidney beans with juice
1 (15-ounce) spicy chili beans with juice
1 (10¾-ounce) can condensed French onion soup
¼ cup cornmeal
1 teaspoon paprika

In a large slow cooker, combine all ingredients; mix well. Cover; cook on high for 2 to 4 hours or until thoroughly heated. Makes 4 to 6 servings.

Barbecued Bean Soup

1 pound dried great Northern beans, soaked overnight, drained, and rinsed
1½ to 2 pounds beef short ribs
¾ cup chopped onion
⅛ teaspoon black pepper
6 cups water
2 teaspoons salt, or to taste
¾ to 1 cup barbecue sauce

In slow cooker, combine beans with ribs, onion, and pepper; add water. Cover and cook on low 10 to 14 hours. Remove ribs and cut meat from bones. Return meat to slow cooker, and stir in barbecue sauce and salt. Cover and cook on high for about 20 minutes more. Makes 8 servings.

Bean and Bacon Soup

4 slices bacon, cooked and crumbled
1¼ cups dried beans, sorted, soaked overnight, and drained
1 onion, chopped
3 cups water
1 (1-ounce) package taco seasoning mix
2 (14-ounce) cans diced tomatoes, undrained

In a slow cooker, combine bacon with dried beans, onion, water, and taco seasoning mix, and mix well to blend. Cover and cook on low for 10 to 12 hours, until beans are tender. Add tomatoes, stir well, and cook on low for 30 to 40 minutes longer until hot. Makes 6 servings.

Bean Soup

2¼ pounds mixed dried beans
4 carrots, chopped
2 onions, chopped
10 cups water
1 teaspoon dried thyme leaves
1 (14-ounce) can diced tomatoes, undrained

Combine all ingredients in a slow cooker except for tomatoes, and stir well to combine. Cover and cook on high for 8 to 10 hours, or until beans are tender. Add tomatoes, stir, cover, and cook on high for 15 to 20 minutes longer until heated. Makes 12 servings.

Beef Broccoli Soup

1½ pounds lean ground beef, browned
3 cups chopped broccoli
2 (4-ounce) cans sliced mushrooms
½ cup chopped celery
1 cup sliced carrots
¼ cup chopped green bell pepper
4 cups tomato juice
½ cup water
¼ teaspoon salt
¼ teaspoon pepper
¼ teaspoon dried thyme
¼ teaspoon dried oregano

Combine all ingredients in a slow cooker. Cover and cook on low for 8 to 9 hours. Makes 6 servings.

Beef Stew

½ cup all-purpose flour
1 teaspoon paprika
Salt and black pepper, to taste
2 pounds well-trimmed beef chuck, cut into 1¼-inch chunks
¼ cup olive oil, divided
1 large onion, chopped
4 small onions, each cut into 6 wedges
4 garlic cloves, minced
¾ teaspoon dried thyme, crumbled
3 bay leaves
1 (14½-ounce) can beef broth, divided
1 (14½-ounce) can stewed tomatoes
1½ cups water
1 pound new potatoes, cut into 1-inch chunks
2 cups butternut squash, peeled, seeded, and cut into 1-inch chunks
2 large carrots, cut into ½-inch slices

In a large bowl, mix the flour, paprika, salt, and pepper. Add beef and toss until coated. Heat 2 tablespoons of the oil over medium-high heat. Cook the beef in small batches for 3 to 4 minutes, until lightly browned on all sides, adding additional oil as needed. Set aside the remaining seasoned flour. Reduce the heat to medium, and add the chopped onion, garlic, thyme, and bay leaves. Pour in ¼ cup of the broth, and cook, scraping with a wooden spoon to loosen any browned bits in the bottom of the pan. Cook, stirring, for 3 to 4 minutes, until the onion is tender, adding additional broth if the pot becomes dry. Stir in the reserved seasoned flour and cook, stirring constantly, for 1 minute.

Place tomatoes, water, potatoes, squash, and carrots into a slow cooker. Transfer beef mixture to slow cooker. Cover and cook for 6 to 8 hours. Makes 8 servings.

Beef Taco Bean Soup

1 (2-pound) rump roast
1 (1-ounce) package taco seasoning mix
1 (15-ounce) can Mexican-style diced tomatoes
1 (4-ounce) can diced green chiles
1 (8-ounce) can tomato sauce
1 onion, chopped
2 beef bouillon cubes
2 (15-ounce) cans red kidney beans, rinsed and drained
Shredded Cheddar cheese

Cut roast into bite-size chunks. Roll in taco seasoning, and add to slow cooker. Then add the tomatoes, chiles, tomato sauce, onion, and bouillon cubes. Cover and cook on low for 6 hours, or until meat is tender. Add beans and cook until heated through, about 30 minutes. Serve topped with cheese. Makes 8 servings.

Best Bean Chili

1 pound lean ground beef, cooked and drained
1 (16-ounce) can red kidney beans
1 (16-ounce) can pinto beans
2¼ pounds tomatoes, diced
1½ cups chopped onion
1 cup chopped green bell pepper
1 teaspoon minced garlic
2½ tablespoons chili powder
1½ teaspoons ground cumin
2 tablespoons brown sugar
1 tablespoon unsweetened cocoa

Combine all ingredients in a slow cooker. Cover and cook on low for 5 to 6 hours. Makes 6 servings.

Black Bean Chili

1 pound pork tenderloin, cubed
2 cups chunky salsa
1 (45-ounce) can black beans, rinsed and drained
½ cup chicken broth
1 red bell pepper, chopped
1 onion, chopped
1 teaspoon cumin
2 teaspoons chili powder
1 teaspoon dried oregano
¼ cup sour cream

Place tenderloin in a slow cooker. Add remaining ingredients except sour cream. Cover and cook on low for 8 hours. Serve with sour cream. Makes 8 servings.

Black Bean Soup with Crab

2 (15-ounce) cans black beans, drained
4 cups chicken broth
1 (15-ounce) can diced tomatoes
½ pound andouille sausage, diced
½ cup diced onions
½ cup diced celery
½ cup diced carrots
1 teaspoon ground cumin
2 bay leaves
Salt and black pepper, to taste
2 cups cooked lump crabmeat
¼ cup chopped fresh cilantro

In a slow cooker, combine beans, broth, tomatoes, sausage, onion, celery, carrots, cumin, bay leaves, salt, and pepper. Mix well. Cover and cook on low for 6 to 8 hours or on high for 3 to 4 hours. Ladle into bowls and garnish with crab and cilantro. Makes 4 servings.

Black Bean Soup with Chipotle Chiles

1 pound dried black beans, sorted, soaked overnight, and drained
1 tablespoon olive oil
2 medium red onions, chopped
1 medium red bell pepper, chopped
1 medium green bell pepper, chopped
4 garlic cloves, minced
4 teaspoons ground cumin
1 tablespoon canned chipotle chiles, chopped
7 cups hot water
2 tablespoons fresh lime juice
2 teaspoons coarse kosher salt
¼ teaspoon black pepper
1 cup plain nonfat yogurt
½ cup seeded plum tomatoes, chopped
¼ cup fresh cilantro, chopped

Heat olive oil in a large nonstick skillet over medium-high heat. Add onions and bell peppers, and sauté until beginning to brown, about 8 minutes. Add garlic and cumin; stir 1 minute. Transfer mixture to a slow cooker. Add beans and chipotles and then hot water. Cover and cook on high until beans are very tender, about 6 hours. Transfer 2 cups bean mixture to blender; purée until smooth. Return purée to remaining soup in slow cooker. Stir in lime juice, salt, and pepper. Ladle soup into bowls. Spoon a dollop of yogurt into each bowl. Sprinkle with tomatoes and cilantro. Makes 8 servings.

Black Bean Mushroom Stew

1 tablespoon extra virgin olive oil
¼ cup mustard seeds
2 tablespoons chili powder
¼ teaspoon ground cardamom
2 medium onions, coarsely chopped
1 pound mushrooms, sliced
½ pound tomatillos, husked, rinsed, and coarsely chopped
¼ cup water
4¼ cups vegetable broth
1 (6-ounce) can tomato paste
2 tablespoons canned chipotle chiles in adobo sauce, minced
1 pound dried black beans, sorted, soaked overnight, and drained
1¼ cups grated Monterey Jack cheese
½ cup low-fat sour cream
½ cup fresh cilantro, chopped
2 limes, cut into wedges

Combine oil, mustard seeds, chili powder, and cardamom in a Dutch oven. Place over high heat, and stir until the spices sizzle, about 30 seconds. Add onions, mushrooms, tomatillos, and ¼ cup water. Cover and cook, stirring occasionally, until vegetables are juicy, 5 to 7 minutes. Uncover and stir often, until the juices evaporate and the vegetables are lightly browned, 10 to 15 minutes. Add broth, tomato paste, and chipotles (with sauce); mix well. Place the beans in a slow cooker. Pour the hot mixture over the beans. Turn heat to high. Cover and cook until the beans are soft, 5 to 8 hours. To serve, ladle the chili into bowls. Garnish each serving with cheese, a dollop of sour cream, a sprinkling of cilantro, and lime wedges. Makes 4 servings.

Black-Eyed Pea Soup

2 cups dried black-eyed peas, sorted, soaked overnight, rinsed, and drained
1 pound smoked turkey sausage, cubed
4 carrots, chopped
½ cup wheat berries
1 cup water
3 (14-ounce) cans beef broth

Combine all ingredients in a slow cooker, cover, and cook on low for 8 to 9 hours, until peas and wheat berries are tender. Makes 8 servings.

Brown Rice and Mushroom Soup

¾ cup long grain brown rice
½ pound mushrooms, finely chopped
1 onion, finely chopped
1 celery stalk, finely chopped
1 teaspoon ground mustard
1 teaspoon black pepper
½ teaspoon salt
¼ teaspoon ground coriander
⅛ teaspoon ground cardamom
⅛ teaspoon ground cinnamon
⅛ teaspoon ground cloves
4¼ cups vegetable or chicken stock
⅓ cup fresh cilantro, chopped
½ cup nonfat plain yogurt or sour cream
3 tablespoons finely chopped scallions

Combine all ingredients except cilantro, yogurt or sour cream, and scallions in a slow cooker. Cover and cook on low 5 to 6 hours, or until rice is tender. Stir in cilantro. Serve topped with a dollop of yogurt and sprinkled with scallions. Makes 4 servings.

Brunswick Stew

1 (2½- to 3-pound) chicken
8 cups water
1 onion, chopped
2 cups cooked and cubed ham
3 potatoes, diced
2 (16-ounce) cans tomatoes, chopped
1 (11-ounce) can lima beans
1 (11-ounce) can whole kernel corn
2 teaspoons salt
½ teaspoon seasoned salt
1 teaspoon sugar
¼ teaspoon black pepper

In a slow cooker, combine chicken with water, onion, ham, and potatoes. Cook covered on low for 4 to 5 hours, or until chicken is done. Remove chicken and pull meat from bones. Return chicken meat to pot. Add tomatoes, beans, corn, salt, seasoned salt, sugar, and pepper. Cover and cook on high 1 hour. Makes 8 servings.

Buffalo Chicken Wing Soup

6 cups milk
3 (10¾-ounce) cans condensed cream of chicken soup
3 cups shredded cooked chicken
1 cup sour cream
¼ to ½ cup hot sauce

Combine all ingredients in a slow cooker. Cover and cook on low for 4 to 5 hours. Makes 8 servings.

Buffalo Stew with Shiitake Mushrooms

1 pound buffalo stewing meat, cubed
12 new potatoes, cut into quarters
½ cup chopped onions
1 (8-ounce) package baby carrots
2 cups fresh Shiitake mushrooms
1 (16-ounce) can tomatoes, diced or whole
1 (14½-ounce) can beef broth
½ cup all-purpose flour
1 tablespoon Worcestershire sauce
1 teaspoon salt
1 teaspoon sugar
1 teaspoon dried marjoram
¼ teaspoon black pepper

Combine all ingredients in a slow cooker. Cook on low 8 to 9 hours. Stir well before serving. Makes 4 servings.

Camper's Stew

1 pound ground beef, browned and drained
2 (16-ounce) cans creamed corn
2 (16-ounce) cans tomatoes
2 (4-ounce) cans boneless chicken
10 ounces ketchup
3 tablespoons Worcestershire sauce
1 tablespoon lemon juice
Dash hot sauce

Combine all ingredients and pour into slow cooker. Cook 3 hours on high or 6 hours on low, stirring occasionally. Makes 8 servings.

Canadian Bacon Soup

1 (16-ounce) package dried lentils, sorted and rinsed
2 (14½-ounce) can vegetable broth
1 (6-ounce) package sliced Canadian bacon, coarsely chopped
2 medium carrots, cut into ½-inch pieces
1 medium potato, peeled and cut into ½-inch cubes
1 medium onion, chopped
1 medium celery stalk, cut into ½-inch pieces
4 cups water
1 teaspoon dried thyme
½ teaspoon salt
¼ teaspoon black pepper

Mix all ingredients in a slow cooker. Cover and cook on low for 8 to 9 hours or on high for 3 to 5 hours, or until lentils are tender. Stir well before serving. Makes 8 servings.

Cauliflower Soup

1 large cauliflower, chopped
2 to 3 slices bacon
6 large mushrooms, sliced
1 vegetable stock cube, crushed
1 onion, chopped
1 (10-ounce) container light sour cream
1 to 2 cups milk, for blending (to desired consistency)
Grated cheese
Crusty bread

Combine cauliflower, bacon, mushrooms, vegetable stock cube, and onion in a slow cooker. Cook on low until bacon is cooked and cauliflower is soft. Add sour cream and stir. Pour into a food processor. Blend on low while slowly adding milk until soup has desired consistency. Pour into serving bowls, top with cheese, and serve with bread. Makes 4 servings.

Cheeseburger Chowder

2 (10¾-ounce) cans Cheddar cheese soup
2 to 3 soup cans of milk
1 large bag frozen hash brown potatoes
1 pound ground beef, browned
1 cup processed American cheese, cubed

Pour ingredients into a slow cooker and heat thoroughly. Makes 4 to 6 servings.

Chicken and Rice Soup

3 onions, chopped
4 celery stalks, sliced
Salt and black pepper, to taste
1 teaspoon dried basil
½ teaspoon dried thyme
½ teaspoon dried sage
1 (20-ounce) package frozen peas
2½ pounds chicken, cut in pieces
5½ cups water
¾ cup rice, uncooked

Place all ingredients, except rice, into a slow cooker in order listed. Cover and cook 1 hour on high; reduce heat to low, and cook for an additional 8 to 9 hours. One hour before serving, remove chicken and cool slightly. Remove meat from bones, and return to slow cooker. Add rice. Cover and cook an additional hour on high. Makes 8 servings.

Chicken Chili

2 pounds boneless, skinless chicken thighs
3 (14-ounce) cans diced tomatoes with chiles and garlic, undrained
2 cups chicken broth
1 (1-ounce) package taco seasoning mix
2 (15-ounce) cans white beans, drained and rinsed

Combine all ingredients in a slow cooker. Cover and cook on low for 7 to 9 hours, or until chicken is tender. Stir well. Makes 8 servings.

Chicken Chowder

½ cup carrots, chopped
1 cup skim milk
1 cup low-sodium chicken broth
⅛ teaspoon white pepper
1 onion, chopped
2 garlic cloves, minced
1 potato, peeled and cubed
½ pound boneless, skinless chicken breasts, cut into 1-inch pieces
2 (15-ounce) cans creamed corn
¼ cup dried potato flakes
½ cup grated Parmesan cheese

Combine all ingredients except potato flakes and cheese in a slow cooker. Cover and cook on low for 5 to 6 hours, or until potatoes are tender and chicken is thoroughly cooked. Add potato flakes and stir well to combine. Cook mixture on high, uncovered, for 5 to 10 minutes, or until chowder has thickened and dried potato flakes have dissolved. Top each serving with cheese. Makes 4 servings.

Chicken Noodle Soup

2½ to 3½ pounds chicken pieces
1 small onion, chopped
1 carrot, chopped
2 celery stalks, chopped
4 cups water
4 cups chicken broth
1 teaspoon seasoned salt
1 teaspoon salt, or to taste, depending on saltiness of broth
¼ teaspoon black pepper
¼ cup chopped fresh parsley
½ teaspoon dried marjoram or basil
1 bay leaf
6 ounces egg noodles

Place all ingredients except noodles in the slow cooker. Cover and cook on low for 5 to 6 hours. Remove chicken and bay leaf from slow cooker; take meat from bones, dice, and return to broth, and add the noodles. Cook another hour, or until noodles are done (about 30 minutes on high). Makes 8 servings.

Chicken Soup

1 tablespoon olive oil
1 tablespoon butter
1 pound boneless, skinless chicken thighs, chopped
2 celery stalks with leaves, sliced
2 large carrots, sliced
1 onion, chopped
1 (14-ounce) can diced tomatoes, undrained
1 (14-ounce) can chicken broth
1 teaspoon dried thyme leaves
½ teaspoon salt
⅛ teaspoon black pepper
1 (9-ounce) package frozen green peas
1 cup refrigerated egg noodles

Heat olive oil and butter in a skillet over medium heat. Add chicken and cook, stirring frequently, for 5 minutes. Place chicken and remaining ingredients, except peas and noodles, in a slow cooker, and stir to mix. Cover and cook on low for 6½ to 7 hours, or until chicken is thoroughly cooked. Stir in peas and noodles, and cook 10 minutes longer, until noodles are tender and soup is thoroughly heated. Makes 8 servings.

Chicken Stew

2 pounds boneless, skinless chicken breasts, cut into 1-inch cubes
3 medium onions, peeled and quartered
2 large carrots, peeled and cut into 1-inch-thick slices
2 potatoes, peeled and cut into 1-inch cubes
2 (14-ounce) cans chicken broth
1 teaspoon celery seed
1 teaspoon dried thyme
½ teaspoon black pepper
1 cup sliced mushrooms
1 cup frozen corn
1 cup frozen peas

In a slow cooker, combine the chicken, onions, carrots, potatoes, and broth. Stir in the celery seeds, thyme, pepper, mushrooms, and corn.

Cover and cook on low about 7 to 9 hours, or on high for 4 to 6 hours, until the chicken is done and the vegetables are tender. Stir in peas and cook another 15 to 30 minutes. Makes 6 servings.

Chicken Stew with Pepper and Pineapple

2 boneless, skinless chicken breasts, cut into 1-inch cubes
4 medium carrots, cut into 1-inch pieces
½ cup chicken broth
1 teaspoon ground ginger
1 tablespoon brown sugar, packed
½ teaspoon ground allspice
½ teaspoon hot sauce
8 ounces canned pineapple chunks, juice drained and reserved
1 tablespoon cornstarch
1 medium green bell pepper, cut into 1-inch pieces

Mix all ingredients except pineapple, pineapple juice, cornstarch, and bell pepper in a slow cooker. Cover and cook on low for 7 to 8 hours, or until vegetables are tender and chicken is no longer pink in center. Mix reserved pineapple juice and cornstarch until smooth. Gradually stir into chicken mixture. Stir in pineapple and bell pepper. Cover and cook on high about 15 minutes or until slightly thickened. Makes 4 servings.

Chicken Taco Soup

1 onion, chopped
1 (16-ounce) can chili beans
1 (15-ounce) can black beans
1 (15-ounce) can whole-kernel corn, drained
1 (8-ounce) can tomato sauce
1½ cups chicken broth
2 (10-ounce) cans diced tomatoes with green chiles, undrained
1 (1-ounce) package taco seasoning
3 boneless, skinless chicken breasts
Shredded Cheddar cheese
Sour cream
Crushed tortilla chips (optional)

Place the onion, chili beans, black beans, corn, tomato sauce, broth, and diced tomatoes in a slow cooker. Add taco seasoning, and stir to blend. Lay chicken breasts on top of the mixture, pressing down slightly until just covered by the other ingredients. Set slow cooker for low heat, cover, and cook for 5 hours. Remove chicken breasts from the soup, and allow to cool. Shred chicken breasts. Stir the shredded chicken back into the soup, and continue cooking for 2 hours. Serve topped with shredded Cheddar cheese, a dollop of sour cream, and crushed tortilla chips, if desired. Makes 6 servings.

Chinese Turkey Stew

1 pound boneless, skinless turkey thighs, cut into 1-inch cubes
1 teaspoon Chinese 5-spice powder
½ teaspoon red pepper flakes
1 tablespoon peanut oil
1 large sweet onion, coarsely chopped
1 cup sliced button mushrooms
2 garlic cloves, minced
2 cups turkey or chicken broth
1 tablespoon cornstarch
1 large red bell pepper, seeded and cut into cubes
2 tablespoons soy sauce
1 tablespoon sesame oil
⅓ cup green onions, chopped
¼ cup fresh cilantro

Toss turkey cubes with 5-spice powder and red pepper flakes in a small bowl. Heat oil in a large skillet over medium heat. Sauté turkey and onion in oil until turkey is brown and onions are soft. Stir in mushrooms and continue to cook until turkey is no longer pink. Add garlic and cook for 30 seconds. Remove from heat.

In a small bowl, combine ¼ cup broth with cornstarch. Cover and refrigerate. Place turkey mixture, remaining broth, bell pepper, and soy sauce in slow cooker. Stir well. Cover and cook on low for 3½ hours or until peppers are soft. Add cornstarch mixture, sesame oil, and green onions, stirring well. Cook an additional 30 to 45 minutes, or until juices become thickened. Ladle into bowls and garnish with cilantro. Makes 4 servings.

This recipe used by permission of the National Turkey Federation.

Chunky Pizza Soup

2 (10¾-ounce) cans tomato soup with basil and oregano
1 (14½-ounce) can Italian-style diced tomatoes, undrained
2 cups water
¼ cup dried rotini pasta
3 slices Canadian bacon, chopped
½ cup croutons
¼ cup shredded mozzarella cheese

Place all ingredients except croutons and cheese in slow cooker. Cook on low for 4 to 6 hours. Place croutons in the bottom of each soup bowl, and top with soup. Sprinkle with mozzarella cheese. Makes 4 servings.

Cottage Stew

1½ pounds lean beef, cut into 1-inch cubes
2 tablespoons all-purpose flour
2 tablespoons butter
2 tablespoons corn oil
2 celery stalks, cut into chunks
1 cup beef stock
½ teaspoon salt
¼ teaspoon black pepper
½ teaspoon dried thyme
½ teaspoon dried marjoram
1 teaspoon dry mustard
2 tablespoons fresh lemon juice
3 tablespoons chopped fresh parsley
Toast, noodles, or potatoes

Coat meat with flour and brown in butter and oil. Combine meat and remaining ingredients, except lemon juice and parsley, and place in a slow cooker. Cover and cook on low 6 to 8 hours. Stir in lemon juice and parsley, and serve with toast, noodles, or potatoes. Makes 4 servings.

Country Chicken Stew

4½ cups chicken broth
3 pounds boneless, skinless chicken breast, cut into 1-inch cubes
1 cup diced sweet onion
2 whole sweet onions, quartered
1 tablespoon butter
½ cup all-purpose flour
2 tablespoons vegetable oil
2 cups frozen peas and carrots
Salt and black pepper, to taste

Place chicken broth, chicken, onions, and butter in a slow cooker. Cover and cook on high 1 hour. Whisk in flour. Add remaining ingredients and cook on low for 5 to 7 hours. Makes 8 servings.

Cowboy Stew

1½ pounds ground beef, browned and drained
Salt and black pepper, to taste
3 to 4 potatoes, cubed
1 onion, chopped
1 (16-ounce) can ranch-style beans

Place all ingredients in a slow cooker. Cook on low for 4 to 6 hours or on high for 1½ to 2 hours. Makes 4 servings.

Crab Stew

2 cups imitation crabmeat, flaked
2 cups whole milk
2 cups half-and-half
3 tablespoons unsalted butter
2 lemon peel strips
½ teaspoon ground mace
Salt and black pepper, to taste
½ cup crushed saltine crackers

Combine all ingredients except crushed crackers in a slow cooker; stir well. Cover and cook on low for 3 to 5 hours. Just before serving, stir in cracker crumbs to thicken. Makes 2 servings.

Cream of Mushroom Soup

12 ounces fresh mushrooms, sliced
2 tablespoons chopped onion
1 tablespoon butter or margarine
3 cups chicken broth
Salt and black pepper, to taste
2 tablespoons all-purpose flour
1 cup sour cream
1 cup half-and-half

In a skillet, sauté mushrooms and onions in butter. Place in slow cooker. Add chicken broth, salt, and pepper; stir well. Cover and cook on low for 6 to 10 hours or on high for 2½ to 3 hours. About 30 minutes before serving, turn slow cooker to high setting. Mix flour and sour cream. Add to slow cooker with half-and-half. Cook until slightly thickened. Makes 4 servings.

Creamy Asparagus Soup

1 pound fresh asparagus, trimmed and cut into ½-inch slices
2 onions, finely minced
2 potatoes, peeled, diced small
2 ribs celery, diced small, with tops included
2 carrots, diced
2 garlic cloves, minced
8 cubes chicken or vegetable bouillon
1 bay leaf
1 tablespoon Worcestershire sauce
¼ cup fresh parsley, chopped, or 1 tablespoon dried parsley
2 sprigs fresh thyme, or 1 teaspoon dried thyme
1 sprig fresh tarragon, chopped, or 1 teaspoon dried tarragon
¼ cup fresh basil, minced, or 2 teaspoons dried basil
1 teaspoon seasoned salt (or to taste)
½ teaspoon white pepper
¼ cup cornstarch
2 cups half-and-half
Sour cream
Chives, chopped

In a slow cooker, combine asparagus, onions, potatoes, celery, carrots, garlic, bouillon, bay leaf, Worcestershire sauce, parsley, thyme, tarragon, basil, seasoned salt, and pepper. Add water to within 1 inch of the top of slow cooker. Cover and cook on high for 6 to 7 hours.

About 2 hours before serving, use a slotted spoon to remove most of the vegetables to a blender. Use a ladle to add some liquid from the slow cooker to the blender. Purée mixture and add back to cooker. Repeat once or twice more as necessary. Add approximately 1 cup of the half-and-half to cooker. Add cornstarch to remaining half-and-half in the carton, close, and shake vigorously. Add mixture to cooker. Continue to cook on high for 1 hour, stirring occasionally. Serve in bowls with a dollop of sour cream and a sprinkling of chopped chives. Makes 4 servings.

Curry Cauliflower Soup

1 pound cauliflower florets, cooked
1 (28-ounce) can diced tomatoes, undrained
1 (14-ounce) vegetable or beef stock
1 onion, chopped and cooked
2 teaspoons curry powder
½ teaspoon garlic powder
⅛ teaspoon ground cumin
Salt and black pepper, to taste

Combine all ingredients in a slow cooker on low heat. Cover and cook about 7 hours, or until cauliflower is tender. Increase heat to high. Add salt and pepper. Cover and cook another 30 minutes. Serve hot or cold. Makes 4 servings.

Dinner Party Stew

2 pound lean beef chuck, cut into 1½- to 2-inch cubes
3 medium onions, sliced
½ cup tomato juice *or VB*
1¾ cups beef broth
1 (4-ounce) can mushrooms
1 tablespoon sugar
½ cup sour cream
salt to taste

Place all ingredients except sour cream in a slow cooker. Cover and cook on low for 8 to 10 hours. Half an hour before serving, stir in sour cream. Makes 4 servings.

Double Corn Stew

3 cups frozen corn
1 onion, chopped
1 (14-ounce) can creamed corn
1 (14-ounce) can chicken broth
⅛ teaspoon black pepper

Combine all ingredients in a slow cooker, and stir gently to mix. Cover and cook on low for 5 to 6 hours, or until corn is tender. Makes 2 servings.

Dutch Chili Soup

1 tablespoon oil
1½ pounds boneless beef round steak, cut into ½-inch cubes
1½ cups water
1 cup chopped onions
1 cup chopped bell pepper
1 cup chopped carrots
2 (14-ounce) cans diced tomatoes
1 (15½-ounce) can tomato sauce
2 (16-ounce) cans dark red kidney beans, drained
½ teaspoon salt
½ teaspoon black pepper
½ teaspoon cayenne pepper
¼ teaspoon garlic powder

Heat oil in a skillet and brown beef. Place in a slow cooker, and add remaining ingredients. Cook 4 to 5 hours on low. Makes 6 to 8 servings.

Dutch Country Soup

½ pound frankfurters, cut into 1-inch pieces
½ cup chopped onion
¼ teaspoon thyme leaves, crushed
2 tablespoons butter or margarine
1 (10¾-ounce) can split pea with ham soup, undiluted
1 cup water
½ cup chicken broth
1 cup diced carrots
Dash black pepper

Place all ingredients in a slow cooker in the order listed. Cover and cook on low for 4 to 6 hours. Makes 4 servings.

Firehouse Chili

3 pounds lean beef, cut into ¼-inch pieces
2 (8-ounce) cans tomato sauce
2 tablespoons onion powder
1 teaspoon garlic powder
¼ cup chili powder
2 tablespoons ground cumin
1 tablespoon paprika
¼ teaspoon ground oregano
½ teaspoon cayenne pepper
½ teaspoon ground white pepper
½ teaspoon salt

Combine all ingredients in a slow cooker. Cover and cook on high for 1 hour. Reduce heat and cook on low for 4 to 6 hours. Makes 6 to 8 servings.

Firehouse Stew

1 pound ground beef
½ pound Italian or breakfast sausage
1 large onion, chopped
3 garlic cloves, minced
½ package sliced smoked sausage or kielbasa
1 head cabbage, chopped
2 (15-ounce) cans diced tomatoes
1 (15-ounce) can tomato puree
¾ cup Worcestershire sauce
Dash sugar
Hot sauce, to taste

Crumble ground beef and Italian sausage together in a large skillet; add onion and garlic, and brown meat. Drain. Pour meat mixture into slow cooker. Add all remaining ingredients. Add a little water if needed. Cook all day in a slow cooker on low. Makes 4 servings.

Fish Chowder

2 celery stalks, chopped
1 green bell pepper, chopped
1 onion, chopped
3 garlic cloves, minced
2 (14-ounce) cans diced tomatoes, undrained
2 cups vegetable juice
1 cup vegetable broth or fish stock
1 tablespoon Worcestershire sauce
½ teaspoon salt
¼ teaspoon crushed red pepper flakes
1 pound firm fish steaks (haddock, swordfish, halibut, salmon), cut into 1-inch pieces
½ cup instant rice
¼ cup chopped fresh parsley
1 teaspoon grated lemon peel
2 tablespoons grated Parmesan cheese

Mix all ingredients except fish, rice, parsley, lemon peel, and cheese in a slow cooker. Cover and cook on low for 6 to 7 hours, or on high for 3 to 4 hours, until vegetables are tender. Stir in fish and rice. Cover and cook on high for 30 to 45 minutes until fish flakes easily when tested with a fork.

Meanwhile, combine parsley, lemon peel, and cheese in a small bowl, and mix to blend. Serve this topping with chowder. Makes 8 servings.

Forgotten Minestrone

1 pound lean beef stew meat
6 cups water
1 (28-ounce) can diced tomatoes, undrained
1 beef bouillon cube
1 medium onion, chopped
2 tablespoons dried parsley
2½ teaspoons salt
1½ teaspoons dried thyme
½ teaspoon black pepper
1 medium zucchini, thinly sliced
1 (16-ounce) can garbanzo beans, drained
1 cup uncooked small elbow or shell macaroni
¼ cup grated Parmesan cheese

In a slow cooker, combine beef, water, tomatoes, bouillon, onion, parsley, salt, thyme, and pepper. Cover and cook on low for 7 to 9 hours, or until meat is tender. Add zucchini, beans, and macaroni; cook on high, covered, 30 to 45 minutes more, or until the vegetables are tender. Sprinkle individual servings with Parmesan cheese. Makes 6 to 8 servings.

French Onion Soup

3 large onions, sliced
2 tablespoons butter or margarine
4 cups water
6 cubes beef bouillon
1 teaspoon Worcestershire sauce
½ teaspoon paprika
Dash black pepper
French bread
Grated Parmesan cheese

In a large frying pan, cook onions in butter until golden. Place onions in a slow cooker. Add water, bouillon cubes, Worcestershire sauce, paprika, and pepper. Cover and cook on low for 4 to 6 hours or on high for 1½ to 2 hours. Serve with a slice of toasted French bread and sprinkle with Parmesan cheese. Makes 4 to 6 servings.

Fresh Asparagus Soup

2 pounds fresh asparagus, trimmed and cut into 1-inch pieces
5 cups chicken broth
4 scallions, chopped
2 medium Russet potatoes, peeled and cut into ½-inch cubes
¼ teaspoon seasoned salt
¼ teaspoon black pepper
Sour cream or plain yogurt and chopped fresh tomatoes, for garnish

In a slow cooker combine asparagus, broth, scallions, and potatoes. Cover and cook on low for 6 to 7 hours, or until the potatoes are tender. Increase the heat to the high setting.

Using a blender or food processor, purée the vegetable solids in batches, with a little of the cooking liquid, until as smooth as possible. Return to the liquid remaining in the slow cooker. Stir in the seasoned salt and pepper. Cover and cook on high 30 minutes longer. Serve garnished with a dollop of sour cream or yogurt and chopped tomatoes. Makes 4 servings.

Fresh Tomato Soup

8 medium tomatoes
1 medium onion, chopped
2 carrots, peeled and thinly sliced
1 garlic clove, crushed
3 cups chicken broth or bouillon
1 tablespoon brown sugar
1 tablespoon chopped fresh basil
1 tablespoon chopped fresh parsley
2 teaspoons Worcestershire sauce
½ teaspoon salt
⅛ teaspoon black pepper

Drop tomatoes in a pan of boiling water for 15 to 20 seconds; immediately rinse with cold water. Remove skins. Cut in half crosswise; squeeze out and discard seeds.

Combine with remaining ingredients in a slow cooker. Cover and cook on low 5 to 6 hours, or until vegetables are very soft. Purée and serve in individual bowls. Makes 4 servings.

Fruit Soup

1½ cups mixed dry fruit
½ cup raisins
1 (8-ounce) can pineapple chunks and juice
1 large Granny Smith apple, cored and chopped
3 cups apple juice, cranberry cocktail, or orange juice
1 cup water
1 tablespoon lemon juice
Cinnamon stick
3 whole cloves
½ teaspoon powdered ginger

Combine all ingredients in a slow cooker and cook on low for 7 to 9 hours. Makes 4 to 6 servings.

Garden Gate Soup

1 to 1½ pounds banana squash, peeled, seeded, and cubed
1 cooking apple, peeled and cubed
1 large sweet potato, peeled and cubed
1 small onion, sliced
1 teaspoon curry powder
2 teaspoons Worcestershire sauce
3 cups apple juice
¼ teaspoon salt
Ground nutmeg

In slow cooker, combine ingredients except nutmeg. Cover and cook on low 6 to 7 hours, or until vegetables are tender. Purée in batches in blender or food processor. Sprinkle with nutmeg. Makes about 6 servings.

Greek Chili

1 pound ground beef, browned and drained
1 tablespoon minced onion
1½ cups water
2 tablespoons chili powder
2 tablespoons cumin powder
3 teaspoons paprika
1 teaspoon dried oregano
¼ teaspoon cayenne pepper
1 teaspoon salt
¼ teaspoon black pepper
3 pieces pita bread, cut in half

Place all ingredients except pita bread in a slow cooker. Cook on high for 1½ to 4 hours or on low for 3½ to 6 hours. To serve, stuff pita halves with ¼ cup chili. Makes 6 servings.

Greek Stew

2 cups peeled and cubed butternut squash
2 cups chopped carrots
2 onions, chopped
1 cup zucchini, chopped
2 garlic cloves, minced
2 (14-ounce) cans diced tomatoes, undrained
1 (15-ounce) can garbanzo beans, rinsed and drained
1 (14-ounce) can vegetable broth
1 teaspoon cumin
½ teaspoon salt
½ teaspoon allspice
¼ teaspoon black pepper
4 cups hot cooked couscous
½ cup feta cheese, crumbled

Combine all ingredients except couscous and cheese in a slow cooker; mix well to combine. Cover and cook on low for 7 to 9 hours, or until all vegetables are tender. Serve with couscous and sprinkle with cheese. Makes 6 servings.

Gumbo

3 tablespoons all purpose flour
3 tablespoons oil
½ pound smoked sausage, cut into ½-inch slices
2 cups frozen cut okra
1 (14½-ounce) can diced tomatoes, undrained
1 large onion, chopped
1 large green bell pepper, chopped
3 garlic cloves, minced
¼ teaspoon cayenne pepper
¼ teaspoon black pepper
1½ cups uncooked regular long-grain white rice
3 cups water
1 (12-ounce) package frozen cooked medium shrimp, rinsed

In small saucepan, combine flour and oil; mix well. Cook, stirring constantly, over medium-high heat for 5 minutes. Reduce heat to medium; cook, stirring constantly, about 10 minutes or until mixture turns reddish brown. Place roux in a slow cooker. Stir in next 8 ingredients. Cover; cook on low for 7 to 9 hours. When ready to serve, cook rice in water as directed on package. Meanwhile, add shrimp to gumbo mixture in slow cooker; mix well. Cover and cook on low for 20 minutes. Serve gumbo over rice. Makes 6 servings.

Ham and Lentil Stew

3 cups ham, cooked and chopped
3 cups carrots, chopped
2 onions, chopped
2 cups dried lentils, sorted and rinsed
2 (10-ounce) cans condensed chicken broth
4 cups water

Combine all ingredients in a slow cooker, and mix to combine. Cover and cook on low for 7 to 9 hours. Makes 4 servings.

Hamburger Stew

1 pound lean ground beef or turkey, cooked and drained
½ cup chopped onion
1 (15-ounce) can small whole potatoes, drained and halved
1 (10-ounce) package frozen mixed vegetables
1 (1-ounce) package beef stew seasoning mix
2 tablespoons all-purpose flour
¾ cup water
¼ cup beef broth

Place all ingredients in a slow cooker and heat on high for 4 to 6 hours or on low 6 to 8 hours. Makes 4 servings.

Italian Sausage Soup

1 pound hot or mild Italian sausage, cut into ½-inch pieces
1 medium onion, coarsely chopped
1 green bell pepper, cut into half rings
1 (14½-ounce) can diced tomatoes with juice
1 (15-ounce) can great northern beans
2 (14-ounce) cans beef broth

Brown the sausage, onion, and green pepper; drain. Pour into slow cooker along with remaining ingredients. Cover and cook on low for 7 to 8 hours. Makes 6 servings.

Italian Wedding Soup

½ pound ground veal
½ pound ground beef
1 egg, slightly beaten
¼ cup breadcrumbs
¼ cup chopped fresh parsley
1 teaspoon dried oregano
1 teaspoon dried basil
½ teaspoon salt
½ teaspoon black pepper
¼ cup grated Parmesan cheese
4 cups chicken stock
½ cup boneless chicken breasts, cooked and shredded
¼ cup finely chopped carrots
¼ cup finely chopped celery
2 cups escarole, cooked and torn into small pieces
2 bay leaves
1 teaspoon garlic powder
½ cup dried pasta

To make meatballs, combine veal, beef, egg, breadcrumbs, parsley, oregano, basil, salt, pepper, and Parmesan cheese. Form into small balls. Bake about 30 minutes on 350° until the meatballs have browned but are still soft. Remove from oven and drain on paper towel.

Combine remaining ingredients in a slow cooker, and add meatballs. Cook on low for 8 hours. Makes 4 to 6 servings.

Irish Stew

2 cups chicken broth
1 teaspoon dried marjoram
1 teaspoon dried parsley
¾ teaspoon salt
½ teaspoon garlic powder
¼ teaspoon black pepper
1¼ pounds white potatoes, peeled and cut into 1-inch pieces
1 pound lean lamb stew meat
1 (8-ounce) package frozen cut green beans
2 small leeks, cut into slices
1½ cups coarsely chopped carrots

Mix together broth, marjoram, parsley, salt, garlic powder, and pepper in a slow cooker. Add potatoes, lamb, green beans, leeks, and carrots. Cover and cook on low for 7 to 9 hours. Makes 4 servings.

Kielbasa Stew

1½ pounds kielbasa sausage, cut into 1-inch pieces
2 pounds sauerkraut, rinsed and drained
3 Granny Smith apples, peeled, cored, and cut into rings
1 onion, cooked and thinly sliced
2¼ pounds red potatoes, quartered
2 cups chicken stock
½ teaspoon caraway seeds
½ cup grated Swiss cheese

Place half the sausage in a slow cooker and top with sauerkraut. Cover with remaining sausage, apple, and onion. Top with potatoes. Add stock and sprinkle with caraway seeds. Cover and cook on high for 4 hours, or until potatoes are tender. Serve sprinkled with cheese. Makes 4 servings.

Meatball Soup

1 (16-ounce) bag frozen, fully cooked meatballs
2 (14-ounce) cans condensed beef broth
1 cup water
2 (14-ounce) cans diced tomatoes with herbs, undrained
1 (16-ounce) bag frozen mixed vegetables

Combine frozen meatballs, broth, water, and tomatoes in a slow cooker. Cover and cook on low for 9 to 10 hours, or until meatballs are tender when pierced with a fork. Stir in the frozen vegetables, and mix well. Cover and cook on high for 1 hour. Makes 4 servings.

Mexican Beef Soup

1 pound beef stew meat
1 (14-ounce) can beef stock
2 cups water
1 (16-ounce) package Mexican-style frozen vegetables
1 (14-ounce) can Mexican-style chunky tomato sauce
1 (16-ounce) can pinto beans, rinsed and drained
2 teaspoons ground cumin
1 (16-ounce) can black beans, rinsed and drained
¼ teaspoon seasoned salt
¼ teaspoon garlic pepper
½ cup sour cream

Combine first seven ingredients in a slow cooker on low heat. Cover and cook 8 to 8½ hours, or until beef is tender. Increase heat to high. Stir in beans, salt, and garlic pepper. Cover and heat another 10 to 20 minutes, until hot. Serve with a dollop of sour cream. Makes 6 servings.

Mexican Chicken Soup

2 pounds boneless, skinless chicken breasts, cubed
3 cups chicken broth
1 (15-ounce) can black soybeans
1 cup chopped tomatoes
1 cup chopped green onion, divided
¼ cup chopped jalapeños
2 garlic cloves, crushed
½ teaspoon ground cumin
½ teaspoon dried Mexican oregano
2 tablespoons lime juice
1 cup shredded Cheddar cheese
½ cup sour cream

Mix chicken, broth, soybeans, tomatoes, ¾ cup green onion, jalapeños, garlic, cumin, and oregano in a slow cooker. Cover and cook on high for 1 hour and then on low for at least 5 hours. Add lime juice and mix well. Place in individual bowls and top evenly with the cheese, sour cream, and reserved green onion. Makes 6 servings.

Moroccan Lentil Stew

1 cup dried lentils, sorted and rinsed
1 pound butternut squash, peeled and cubed
10 small new red potatoes, cubed
1 onion, chopped
4 garlic cloves, minced
2 (14-ounce) cans diced tomatoes, undrained
1 tablespoon curry powder
½ teaspoon salt
⅛ teaspoon white pepper
⅛ teaspoon red pepper flakes
2 cups water
1 (8-ounce) package frozen cut green beans, thawed

Combine all ingredients except green beans in a slow cooker. Cover and cook on low for 8 to 10 hours, until lentils, squash, and potatoes are tender when tested with knife. Increase heat to high setting. Stir in thawed green beans, cover, and cook for 10 to 15 minutes until mixture is thoroughly heated and beans are tender. Makes 6 servings.

Moroccan Soup

2 pounds turkey breast or thighs, cut in ½-pound chunks and skin removed
1½ cups lentils, rinsed
1 cup chopped onion
1 cup chopped celery
2 tablespoons tomato paste
1 teaspoon ground turmeric
½ teaspoon ground cinnamon
7 cups turkey or chicken broth
2 tablespoons fresh lemon juice
Salt and black pepper, to taste

Place thighs or breasts in a slow cooker. Add lentils, onion, celery, tomato paste, turmeric, cinnamon, and turkey broth; stir well. Cover and cook until turkey is tender, 3 to 5 hours on high or 7 to 9 hours on low. Remove turkey from soup and tear from bones in bite-sized pieces; return to soup. Heat mixture to 160°. Season to taste with lemon juice, salt, and pepper. Makes 8 servings.

This recipe used by permission of the National Turkey Federation.

Pork and Black Bean Stew

1½ pounds pork tenderloin, cut into 1-inch pieces
½ cup all-purpose flour
1 teaspoon chili powder
½ teaspoon salt
¼ teaspoon black pepper
2 tablespoons olive oil
½ pound pork sausage
1½ cups onion, chopped
1 (10¾-ounce) can condensed chicken broth
¼ cup fresh chopped parsley
3 large garlic cloves, minced
1 (4-ounce) can chopped mild green chiles (optional)
Dash dried oregano
2 (15-ounce) cans black beans, drained and rinsed
1 cup frozen corn kernels
1 large red bell pepper, chopped
2 plum tomatoes, diced
1 teaspoon lemon juice
Salt and black pepper, to taste
Cornbread
Diced tomato and green onion, for garnish (optional)

Toss pork in a food storage bag with flour, chili powder, salt, and pepper. Heat olive oil in a large skillet. Add coated pork to the skillet along with any remaining flour; brown on all sides. Pour into a slow cooker. Add pork sausage and onions to skillet and brown lightly; add to cooker. Add the condensed chicken broth, parsley, and garlic. Cook on low for 9 to 11 hours or on high for 4½ to 6 hours.

About 2 hours before done (or 1 hour if cooking on high), add the chiles, oregano, black beans, corn, bell pepper, tomatoes, and lemon juice. Continue cooking.

Taste and adjust seasoning. Serve in bowls, with cornbread and a garnish of tomatoes and green onions. Makes 6 to 8 servings.

Potato Cheese Soup

8 potatoes, cubed
1 tablespoon chopped chives
1½ cups chopped celery
⅓ cup chopped fresh parsley
½ cup chopped onion
¼ teaspoon paprika
¼ teaspoon celery seed
1 teaspoon dried savory
½ teaspoon salt
Water
1 cup milk
2 tablespoons all-purpose flour
2 tablespoons butter
2½ cups grated Cheddar cheese

Combine first 9 ingredients in a slow cooker; add water to cover. Cook on high for 1 hour. Turn heat to low, and cook 4 to 5 hours, or until potatoes are done. Combine milk and flour thoroughly. In a small saucepan, melt butter over medium heat. Add flour mixture slowly, and stir constantly 3 to 4 minutes. Add cheese; stir until melted. Turn slow cooker to high setting. Add cheese mixture to soup, and cook until slightly thickened. Makes 12 servings.

Potato Chowder

4 large potatoes, cubed
1 (5-ounce) package scalloped potato mix
4 cups chicken broth
2 onions, chopped
2 cups half-and-half
⅓ cup all-purpose flour
⅛ teaspoon white pepper

In a slow cooker, combine potatoes and sauce from scalloped potato mix with chicken broth and onions. Stir well to blend. Cover and cook on low for 7 hours. In medium bowl, mix together cream and flour with a wire whisk until smooth. Stir this mixture into the slow cooker very slowly, stirring constantly until well blended. Cover and cook on low for 1 more hour, stirring occasionally, until soup thickens. Makes 5 servings.

Potato Soup

6 medium potatoes, diced
3 carrots, sliced
3 ribs celery, chopped
½ cup chopped onion
6 cups chicken broth
1 teaspoon dried parsley
⅔ cup evaporated milk

In a slow cooker, combine all ingredients except evaporated milk. Cover and cook on low for 6½ to 9 hours. Add evaporated milk 30 minutes before soup is done. Makes 6 to 8 servings.

Prima Donna Chili

2 pounds ground beef
1 onion, finely diced
3 garlic cloves, minced
1 (14½-ounce) can diced tomatoes
2 (14½-ounce) cans diced tomatoes, Italian-style
1 (15-ounce) can kidney beans
1 (15-ounce) can pinto beans
1 (8-ounce) can tomato sauce
1 cup water
1 tablespoon hot pepper sauce
2 tablespoons chili powder
2 tablespoons sugar
1 tablespoon ground cumin
1 teaspoon salt
1 teaspoon black pepper

Brown the ground beef with the onion and garlic until the onion is clear. Place the ground beef mixture in a slow cooker. Add the remaining ingredients. Cover and cook on low for 6 to 8 hours. Makes 6 servings.

Prospector's Stew

2 to 3 large potatoes, peeled and cut into bite-sized pieces
1 pound kielbasa, sliced
2 (15-ounce) cans green beans, drained
1 small onion, quartered
1 clove garlic, minced
2 (10¾-ounce) cans cream of mushroom soup
1 cup shredded Cheddar cheese

Place all ingredients except cheese in a slow cooker. Cover and cook on low for 6 to 10 hours. Sprinkle with Cheddar cheese before serving. Makes 6 servings.

Pumpkin Soup

1 tablespoon butter
1 cup chopped onion
2 teaspoons minced garlic
2 pounds ham, cut into 1-inch cubes
3 (29-ounce) cans pumpkin purée
4 cups chicken broth
⅔ cup cream
1 teaspoon fresh thyme
1 teaspoon black pepper
1 teaspoon dried rosemary

Melt the butter in a skillet over medium heat. Cook the onion and garlic until soft. Combine the onion and garlic and remaining ingredients in a slow cooker set to low; cook 8 to 10 hours. Makes 6 servings.

Ravioli Stew

2 cups sliced carrots
1 onion, chopped
2 garlic cloves, minced
2 (14-ounce) cans vegetable broth
2 (14-ounce) cans Italian style diced tomatoes, undrained
1 (18-ounce) can cannellini beans, rinsed and drained
1 teaspoon dried basil
⅛ teaspoon black pepper
1 (9-ounce) package refrigerated cheese-stuffed ravioli
½ cup grated Parmesan cheese

Combine all ingredients except ravioli and cheese in a slow cooker. Cover and cook on low for 6 hours until carrots are tender. Increase heat to high, and stir in ravioli. Cover and cook for 6 to 8 minutes until ravioli are tender. Sprinkle with cheese and serve. Makes 4 servings.

Roman Stew

3 pounds beef stew meat
3 tablespoons olive oil
4 garlic cloves
2 cups sliced celery
1 medium onion, peeled and sliced
1 teaspoon salt
1¼ teaspoons ground cinnamon
¼ teaspoon ground cloves
1¼ teaspoons black pepper
⅛ teaspoon ground allspice
⅛ teaspoon ground nutmeg
1 (14½-ounce) can diced tomatoes, undrained
1 cup beef broth

In a large skillet, brown the beef in the oil over medium-high heat. Transfer the beef to slow cooker. Add garlic, celery, and onion, sprinkle the salt, cinnamon, cloves, pepper, allspice, and nutmeg over the beef and vegetables. Pour tomatoes and broth over beef and vegetables. Cover and cook on low for 7 to 8 hours. Makes 8 servings.

Rustic Stew

2 to 3 pounds boneless, skinless chicken breasts
1 tablespoon butter
2 teaspoons minced garlic
4 cups chicken broth
1¼ pounds small red potatoes, halved
1 cup baby carrots
1 cup sliced celery
½ cup small boiling onions
2 teaspoons dried thyme
1 cup portobello mushrooms

Brown chicken in a skillet with butter and garlic. Pour broth in a slow cooker. Add potatoes, carrots, celery, onion, thyme, and mushrooms. Place chicken on top. Cover and cook on low for 7 to 9 hours. Makes 6 servings.

Savory Tomato Beef Stew

3 tablespoons all-purpose flour
½ teaspoon paprika
1½ pounds beef stew meat
1 onion, diced
1 (13-ounce) can crushed tomatoes
3 tablespoons white vinegar
1 tablespoon Worcestershire sauce
2 tablespoons ketchup
½ teaspoon salt

Combine flour and paprika in a plastic bag. Add beef and shake gently until meat is coated. Place the beef and onion in a slow cooker, reserving the leftover flour mixture. Combine all other ingredients except the salt with the flour in a bowl. Pour over the meat. Cover and cook for 8 to 10 hours on low or 4 to 5 hours on high. During last 30 minutes of cooking, add the salt. Makes 4 to 6 servings.

Seafood Chowder

2 celery stalks, chopped
1 red bell pepper, chopped
1 medium onion, chopped
2 garlic cloves, chopped
2 (14-ounce) cans diced tomatoes
½ cup vegetable stock
1 tablespoon Worcestershire sauce
½ teaspoon salt
¼ teaspoon cayenne pepper
¼ cup long-grain instant white rice
1 pound firm, fleshy fish, cut into 1-inch cubes
3 tablespoons chopped fresh parsley

Mix together all ingredients except fish, rice, and parsley. Cover and cook on low for 7 hours or on high for 3 hours. For the last 30 minutes of cooking, stir in rice, fish, and parsley. Makes 6 servings.

Shrimp Stew

1 onion, chopped
1 green bell pepper, chopped
3 celery stalks, chopped
2 (14-ounce) cans diced tomatoes
1 (8-ounce) can tomato sauce
1 (6-ounce) can tomato paste
1 teaspoon lemon juice
¼ cup chopped fresh parsley
1½ pounds shrimp, peeled and deveined
¾ cup all-purpose flour
½ cup water
Cooked rice

Put onion, bell pepper, and celery into slow cooker. Pour tomatoes, tomato sauce, and tomato paste over all. Add lemon juice and parsley, and cook on low for 6 hours. Add shrimp and cook on high for 1 hour. Mix flour and water together, and pour into slow cooker; stir. Remove lid, and cook on high for an additional 30 minutes. Serve over rice. Makes 4 to 6 servings.

Southwestern Beef Soup

1 pound boneless beef round, cut into thin strips
1 tablespoon vegetable oil
1 onion, chopped
2 garlic cloves, minced
1 (14-ounce) can diced tomatoes
1 cup frozen whole-kernel corn
1 (4-ounce) can diced green chiles
2 tablespoons chopped fresh cilantro
1 cup beef broth
½ teaspoon ground cumin
2 corn tortillas, in strips
2 tablespoons chopped green onion

Stir-fry beef in hot oil for 2 to 3 minutes. Place all ingredients except tortilla strips and green onion into a slow cooker. Cover and cook for 6 to 8 hours on low. Place tortilla strips in soup bowls, cover with soup. Sprinkle with green onion. Makes 4 servings.

Spinach, Chicken, and Wild Rice Soup

3 cups water
1 (14-ounce) can reduced-sodium chicken broth
1 (10¾-ounce) can cream of chicken soup
⅔ cup wild rice, rinsed and drained
½ teaspoon dried thyme, crushed
¼ teaspoon black pepper
1 pound chicken or turkey, cooked and chopped
2 cups coarsely chopped fresh spinach

In a slow cooker, combine water, broth, cream of chicken soup, uncooked wild rice, thyme, and pepper. Cover and cook on low for 7 to 8 hours or on high for 3½ to 4 hours. To serve, stir in chicken and spinach. Makes 4 servings.

Split Pea Soup

8 cups chicken stock
2 cups split peas
1 medium onion, diced
1 large carrot, chopped
1 celery stalk, chopped
1 ham hock
1 teaspoon bacon drippings
Black pepper, to taste

Combine all ingredients in a slow cooker, and cook on low for 8 to 10 hours. Remove ham hock and debone. Purée soup and then add ham back in. Makes 6 servings.

Sweet and Sour Chicken Stew

1 pound boneless, skinless chicken breasts, cut into 1-inch pieces
1 (9-ounce) package baby carrots
1 onion, chopped
1 (14-ounce) can condensed chicken broth
1½ cups water
1 tablespoon finely chopped fresh ginger
1 (10-ounce) jar sweet and sour simmer sauce
1 (8-ounce) can pineapple chunks, drained, juice reserved
2 tablespoons cornstarch
1 red bell pepper, chopped
1 yellow bell pepper, chopped
1 cup thin egg noodles

Combine chicken, carrots, onion, broth, water, ginger, and sweet and sour sauce in a slow cooker. Cover and cook on low for 8 hours, until vegetables are tender. Mix reserved pineapple juice with cornstarch until smooth and stir into chicken mixture. Stir in pineapple, bell peppers, and egg noodles. Cover and cook on high for 25 to 35 minutes, or until pasta is tender and vegetables are heated through. Makes 6 to 8 servings.

Tex-Mex Beef Stew

1 pound beef chuck pot roast, trimmed and cut into 1-inch pieces
1 tablespoon olive oil
2 (14-ounce) cans Mexican diced tomatoes, undrained
2 onions, chopped
3 garlic cloves, minced
2 (15-ounce) cans pinto beans, rinsed and drained
3 cups beef broth
1 (6-ounce) can tomato paste
1 (4-ounce) can chopped green chiles, undrained
1 tablespoon chili powder
¼ teaspoon red pepper flakes
¼ teaspoon ground cloves
¼ teaspoon ground cinnamon
½ teaspoon salt
⅛ teaspoon black pepper
1 zucchini, chopped
2 yellow bell peppers, chopped

Sauté meat in the olive oil over medium heat in a nonstick skillet until browned, about 5 to 6 minutes. Drain well. Place in a slow cooker. Add remaining ingredients except zucchini and peppers. Cover and cook on low for 10 to 12 hours until beef is cooked and vegetables are tender.

Turn heat to high; add zucchini and peppers. Cover and cook for 20 to 30 minutes until thoroughly heated. Makes 6 to 8 servings.

Thai Curry Seafood Stew

1 tablespoon red curry paste
1 (13½-ounce) can unsweetened coconut milk
1 (2-inch) piece fresh ginger, grated
Juice of 2 limes, divided
½ cup water
1½ cups shredded carrots
1½ cups shredded purple cabbage
1 Vidalia onion, coarsely chopped
5 garlic cloves, peeled and coarsely chopped
2 tablespoons oyster sauce
Salt, to taste
1 bunch Thai basil, chopped
¼ cup butter, divided
4 tablespoons olive oil, divided
1½ pounds clams, rinsed
1 pound large shrimp, peeled and deveined
1 pound sea scallops
Cooked rice

Place curry paste in bottom of slow cooker, and add coconut milk. Stir with whisk to combine. Blend in ginger, juice of 1 lime, and water. Add vegetables. Cook for 3 hours on high or 6 hours on low. During the last 30 minutes of cooking, add additional lime juice, oyster sauce, salt, and most of basil.

Melt half of the butter, and pour in half of the olive oil into a heavy sauté pan fitted with a lid. Cook clams until they open, discarding any that do not. Place in slow cooker.

Sauté shrimp and scallops in remaining butter and olive oil in pan on medium heat until shrimp turn pink and scallops turn golden brown. Add to rest of dish. Season to taste. Garnish with more freshly torn Thai basil. Serve over rice. Makes 8 servings.

Thick and Spicy Chili

1½ pounds ground beef
1 small onion, chopped
3 (16-ounce) cans pinto beans
1 (8-ounce) can tomato sauce
1 (6-ounce) can tomato paste
½ teaspoon cayenne pepper
1 (8-ounce) can sliced mushrooms
⅛ cup sugar
1 teaspoon chili powder
1 teaspoon garlic powder
1 teaspoon seasoning salt

Put all of the ingredients in a slow cooker. Cover and cook on low for 8 to 10 hours or on high for 4 to 6 hours. Makes 8 servings.

Turkey Chili and Beans

1 pound ground turkey
2 (14-ounce) cans whole peeled tomatoes, drained
2 (14-ounce) cans kidney beans, drained and rinsed
1 (14-ounce) can black beans, drained and rinsed
1 (12-ounce) can tomato sauce
1 cup finely chopped celery
1 cup finely chopped carrot
1 cup finely chopped onion
3 tablespoons chili powder
4 teaspoons ground cumin
2 teaspoons cayenne pepper
1 teaspoon salt
½ cup water
½ cup shredded Monterey Jack cheese

Cook ground turkey in a heavy skillet over medium heat until the pink color disappears. Place turkey and all other ingredients except cheese in a slow cooker. Mix well and cook on high for 7 hours. Garnish with cheese. Makes 8 servings.

This recipe used by permission of the National Turkey Federation.

Turkey Tortilla Soup

2 skinless turkey thighs
1 (15-ounce) can diced tomatoes
1 onion, diced
1 clove garlic, crushed
1 jalapeño, seeded and chopped
4 cups chicken stock
Salt, to taste
Tortilla chips
½ cup fresh cilantro, chopped

Combine all ingredients except chips and cilantro in a slow cooker. Cover and cook on low 7 to 8 hours, until turkey is tender.

Remove turkey, cool slightly, and remove meat from bones. Chop turkey meat and divide among soup bowls. Process remaining soup mixture in a blender or food processor until puréed. Pour over turkey in soup bowls. Serve with tortilla chips and cilantro. Makes 4 servings.

Tuscan Sausage and Bean Soup

¾ pound Italian sausage links, cut into ½-inch pieces
1 (16-ounce) can great northern beans
1 (14-ounce) can whole Italian style tomatoes
1 (14-ounce) can beef broth
4 cups water
1 garlic clove, minced
½ teaspoon dried Italian seasoning
2 cups sliced yellow summer squash or zucchini
1 medium onion, chopped
1 (10-ounce) package frozen chopped spinach, thawed
Grated Parmesan cheese

In a slow cooker, combine the Italian sausage, beans, tomatoes, beef broth, water, garlic, and seasoning. Cook covered on high for 8 to 10 hours. Add vegetables during last hour of cooking. Sprinkle with Parmesan cheese before serving. Makes 4 servings.

Vegetable and Barley Soup

½ cup sliced zucchini
¼ cup barley
2 tablespoons dried lentils
8 cups water
¼ cup beef broth
½ cup tomato paste
2 tablespoons Dijon mustard
2 tablespoons minced garlic
½ cup chopped red onion
½ cup chopped yellow onion
6 tablespoons chopped sun-dried tomatoes
1 cup chopped red bell pepper
2 tablespoons olive oil
2 cups sliced button mushrooms
1 cup diced tomatoes
1 cup sliced celery
1¼ cups sliced carrots
½ cup quartered green beans
½ cup sliced yellow squash
3 bay leaves
¾ teaspoon ground white pepper
½ teaspoon kosher salt
1½ teaspoons dried thyme
⅜ teaspoon dried dill
1⅛ teaspoons dried oregano
¼ cup chopped parsley
¼ cup chopped fresh basil

Place all ingredients in a slow cooker, and cook on high 4 to 6 hours or on low 6 to 8 hours. Makes 8 servings.

Vegetable and Beef Soup

1½ pounds beef stew meat
1 green bell pepper, chopped
1 onion, chopped
2 garlic cloves, minced *(one teaspoon)*
1 cup frozen green beans
1 cup frozen corn
2 (14-ounce) cans beef broth
2 (14-ounce) cans diced tomatoes with roasted garlic, undrained
1 (8-ounce) can tomato sauce
⅔ cup uncooked pearl barley
1½ cups water
½ teaspoon salt
½ teaspoon dried ~~thyme~~ leaves *parsley/basil*
¼ teaspoon black pepper

Mix all ingredients in a slow cooker. Cover and cook on low for 8 to 9 hours or high for 4 to 5 hours, until vegetables, stew meat, and barley are tender, stirring once during cooking time. Makes 6 servings.

Vegetable Minestrone

2 carrots, sliced
2 celery stalks, chopped
1 onion, chopped
2 garlic cloves, minced
1 cup sliced mushrooms
2 (14-ounce) cans diced tomatoes, undrained
4 cups vegetable broth or stock
4 cups tomato juice
1 tablespoon dried basil
1 teaspoon salt
½ teaspoon dried basil leaves
⅛ teaspoon black pepper
1½ cups dried rotini pasta
Parmesan cheese, freshly grated

Mix all ingredients except pasta and cheese in a slow cooker. Cover and cook on low for 7 to 8 hours, until vegetables are tender. Stir in pasta. Cover and cook on high setting for 15 to 25 minutes until pasta is tender. Sprinkle each serving with Parmesan cheese. Makes 12 servings.

Vegetarian Chili

1 onion, chopped
1 green bell pepper, chopped
2 celery stalks, chopped
2 garlic cloves, chopped
1 (19-ounce) can black bean soup
1 (15-ounce) can kidney beans, rinsed and drained
1 (15-ounce) can garbanzo beans, rinsed and drained
1 (16-ounce) can vegetarian baked beans
1 (14½-ounce) can diced tomatoes in purée
1 (15-ounce) can whole-kernel corn, drained
1 tablespoon chili powder, or to taste
1 tablespoon dried parsley
1 tablespoon dried oregano
1 tablespoon dried basil

In a slow cooker, combine all ingredients. Cook for at least 2 hours on high. Makes 12 servings.

White Chicken Chili

1 large onion, chopped
2 garlic cloves, finely chopped
1 (14½-ounce) can chicken broth
1 teaspoon ground cumin
1 teaspoon dried oregano
½ teaspoon salt
¼ teaspoon hot sauce
6 skinless chicken thighs
2 (16-ounce) cans great northern beans, rinsed and drained
1 (15-ounce) can whole-kernel corn, drained
3 tablespoons lime juice
2 tablespoons chopped fresh cilantro

Mix onion, garlic, broth, cumin, oregano, salt, and hot sauce in a slow cooker. Add chicken. Cover and cook on low for 4 to 5 hours, or until chicken is tender. Remove chicken, use forks to debone, and shred chicken into pieces. Return chicken to slow cooker. Stir in beans, corn, lime juice, and cilantro. Cover and cook on low for 15 to 20 minutes, or until beans and corn are hot. Makes 8 servings.

White Turkey Chili

4 cups turkey, cooked and chopped
1 cup chopped onion
1 cup chopped celery
2 (15½-ounce) cans great Northern beans, drained
2 (11-ounce) cans white shoepeg corn, undrained
1 (4-ounce) can diced green chiles
1 quart turkey broth
1 teaspoon ground cumin
½ cup grated mozzarella cheese

Place all ingredients except cheese in a slow cooker. Mix well and cook on low for 6 to 8 hours. Sprinkle with mozzarella. Makes 8 servings.

This recipe used by permission of the National Turkey Federation.

Wild Rice Soup

¾ pound bacon, browned, drained, and crumbled
1 onion, diced
2 (8-ounce) cans mushrooms, drained
3 (10¾-ounce) cans cream of potato soup
1 pint half-and-half
1¾ cups water
½ cup wild rice, rinsed
2 cups shredded American cheese
Salt and black pepper, to taste

Combine ingredients in a slow cooker. Cook on low 4 to 6 hours, until rice is done. Makes 4 servings.

Yellow Pea Chowder

1 pound package dried yellow split peas, sorted and rinsed
4 cups water
1 (10-ounce) can condensed chicken broth
1 cup sliced chorizo sausage
1 cup carrot, chopped
¼ teaspoon salt
⅛ teaspoon black pepper
1 (11-ounce) can corn with red and green peppers, drained

Combine all ingredients except corn in a slow cooker and stir to mix. Cover and cook on low for 7 to 9 hours. Stir in corn, increase, heat to high, cover, and cook 10 minutes longer. Makes 4 servings.

Zucchini and Potato Soup

2 pounds potatoes, peeled and cut into 1-inch cubes
2 pounds zucchini, cut into 1-inch cubes
2 medium onions
5 cups chicken stock
½ teaspoon nutmeg
Yogurt (optional)

Place all of the ingredients into slow cooker. Cover and cook for 8 to 10 hours on low. When ready to serve, purée soup in a blender. Top with a dollop of yogurt if desired. Makes 8 to 10 servings.

BEEF, LAMB, AND PORK

Acapulco Flank Steak

1½ to 2 pounds beef flank steak, well trimmed
6 fresh tomatillos, husks and stems removed
1 (15-ounce) can whole baby corn, drained
½ teaspoon salt
¼ teaspoon black pepper
¼ cup chopped fresh cilantro
1 small red onion, thinly sliced
¼ cup beef broth

Place steak in a slow cooker. Chop tomatillos and add to steak. Top with baby corn, salt, pepper, cilantro, and onion. Pour in broth. Cover and cook on low about 6 hours, or until steak is tender. Slice steak crosswise into strips. Spoon vegetables and sauce over sliced steak. Makes 6 to 7 servings.

All-Day-Long Beef

1 yellow onion, sliced and separated into rings
3 carrots, diced
2 celery stalks, diced
1 green bell pepper, chopped
1½ pounds beef roast, cut into serving-size pieces
½ teaspoon black pepper
2 garlic cloves, minced
½ package onion soup mix
2 teaspoons Worcestershire sauce
1 teaspoon steak sauce
½ cup water
½ cup tomato juice

Place onion, carrots, celery, and bell pepper into bottom of a slow cooker. Sprinkle the beef pieces with fresh ground black pepper, minced garlic, and the onion soup mix. Place on top of the vegetables. Mix the steak sauce and Worcestershire sauce in a small bowl with water and tomato juice. Pour over the meat. Cover and cook on low for 7 to 9 hours. Makes 4 servings.

Appley Kielbasa

2 pounds fully cooked kielbasa sausage
¾ cup brown sugar
1 cup chunky applesauce
2 garlic cloves, minced

Cut kielbasa into 1-inch pieces, and combine with remaining ingredients in a slow cooker. Cover and cook on low for 6 to 8 hours, until thoroughly heated. Makes 12 servings.

Baby Back Ribs

¼ cup chili powder
¼ cup dark brown sugar
4 (1-pound) racks baby back ribs
¼ cup barbecue sauce

Mix chili powder and brown sugar; rub on ribs. Curl racks, meaty side out; stand upright on thick ends in a slow cooker. Cover and cook on low for 7 to 8 hours, or on high for 3 to 3½ hours, or until meat is very tender.

Remove ribs to cutting board. Let rest for 5 minutes, and brush with barbecue sauce. Makes 8 servings.

Barbecue Sandwich

1½ pounds boneless beef round steak
½ teaspoon salt
¼ teaspoon black pepper
2 cups purchased coleslaw mix
½ cup barbecue sauce

Trim beef and cut into 1-inch pieces; sprinkle with salt and pepper. In a medium bowl, combine coleslaw mix and barbecue sauce. Layer beef and coleslaw mixture in a slow cooker. Cover and cook on low for 8 to 9 hours, until beef is tender. Stir well with fork so that beef falls apart. Serve on crusty sandwich buns. Makes 4 servings.

Beach Boy Pot Roast

1 (2- to 3-pound) beef roast
Slivers of garlic
1 jar peperoncini peppers

Cut some slits in roast and insert garlic slivers. Place beef in a slow cooker. Dump peppers and all of the juice on top. Cook all day on low, at least 12 hours. Slice and serve, or make hoagies. Makes 6 to 8 servings.

Beef and Broccoli

¾ pound thin beef strips
2 cups fresh broccoli flowerets
1 package gravy mix
1 cup water

Place beef and broccoli in the bottom of a slow cooker. Mix together gravy mix and water. Pour over the top. Cover and cook on low for 6 to 8 hours. Makes 2 servings.

Beef and Black-Eyed Peas

1 (16-ounce) package dried black-eyed peas, sorted, soaked overnight, and drained
3 pounds beef chuck roast, cut into 2-inch cubes
4 carrots, peeled and chopped
1 (10-ounce) can condensed bean and bacon soup
3 cups water
¼ teaspoon black pepper

Combine all ingredients in a slow cooker. Cover and cook on low for 9 to 10 hours or until peas are tender and beef is done. Makes 8 servings.

Beef and Potatoes

3 to 4 potatoes, thinly sliced
1 teaspoon salt
½ teaspoon black pepper
1 pound ground beef, browned
1 medium onion, chopped
1 (10½-ounce) can spaghetti sauce
2 tablespoons butter, melted

Put potatoes in the bottom of a slow cooker. Sprinkle with salt and pepper. Add remaining ingredients. Cover and cook on low for 8 to 10 hours. Makes 4 servings.

Cajun Beef and Potatoes

3 tablespoons Caribbean jerk marinade
1½ pounds round steak, trimmed and cut into 1-inch pieces
4 potatoes, cut into chunks
⅓ cup all-purpose flour
1 (14-ounce) can diced tomatoes, undrained

Combine marinade and beef in a large glass dish and stir to coat. Let stand for 15 to 30 minutes. Place potatoes in a slow cooker. Add flour to beef, mix to coat, and place on top of potatoes. Add tomatoes. Cover and cook on low for 8 to 9 hours, until beef and potatoes are tender. Makes 4 servings.

Cantonese Pork

1½ pounds pork steak, cubed
1 green onion, sliced
1 onion, sliced
1 (4-ounce) can mushrooms, drained
1 (8-ounce) can tomato sauce
2 tablespoons brown sugar
2 teaspoons Worcestershire sauce
1½ tablespoons vinegar
Cooked rice

Put all of the ingredients except the rice into a slow cooker. Cover and cook on low for 8 to 10 hours or on high for 4 to 6 hours. Serve over rice. Makes 4 servings.

Caribbean Ribs

1 teaspoon black pepper
½ teaspoon ground allspice
1 teaspoon dry mustard
1 teaspoon salt
3 pounds pork loin back ribs, cut into 4-inch pieces
½ cup water
1½ cups barbecue sauce

Combine all spices in a small bowl. Rub ribs with spice mixture. Place in a slow cooker and pour water over. Cover and cook on low for 8 to 9 hours, or until ribs are tender when pierced with a fork.

Remove ribs from slow cooker, and discard cooking liquid. Put ribs back in slow cooker, and add barbecue sauce. Cover and cook on low for 1 hour. Makes 6 to 8 servings.

Cheeseburgers

1 pound extra lean ground beef
3 tablespoons ketchup
2 teaspoons yellow mustard
2 cups cubed processed American cheese
10 hamburger buns

Cook ground beef in a large skillet until thoroughly done, about 5 minutes. Stir frequently to break meat up into small pieces. Drain beef thoroughly.

Put cooked beef in a slow cooker with ketchup and mustard; mix well. Top with cubed cheese. Cover and cook on low for 3 to 4 hours. Stir beef mixture gently. Serve in hamburger buns. Makes 10 servings.

Cheesy Sausage and Tortellini

1 pound Italian sausage, casings removed
1 (26-ounce) jar pasta sauce
1 (14-ounce) can diced tomatoes with Italian seasonings, undrained
1 (9-ounce) package refrigerated cheese tortellini
1 cup grated Parmesan cheese

Cook sausage in a heavy skillet over medium heat until browned, about 10 minutes. Stir sausage frequently to break up as it cooks. Drain well and place in a slow cooker. Add pasta sauce and tomatoes, and stir well. Cover and cook on low 7 to 8 hours. Then stir in tortellini, cover again, and cook on low for 30 to 40 minutes, until pasta is tender and heated. Sprinkle with cheese, and let stand 5 minutes before serving. Makes 4 servings.

Chili Beef Sandwiches

1 (3-pound) boneless beef chuck roast, well trimmed
1 (1-ounce) package taco seasoning mix
½ cup barbecue sauce
8 kaiser rolls, split and toasted

Brown beef on all sides in heavy skillet over medium-high heat; transfer to a slow cooker. Sprinkle with seasoning mix, and pour sauce over; cover and cook on low for 8 to 10 hours. Remove beef and shred; return to slow cooker. Make sandwiches with kaiser rolls. Makes 8 servings.

Chuck Roast au Gratin

6 potatoes, peeled and cut into quarters
3½ pounds boned chuck roast
1 tablespoon dried chives, chopped (optional)
2 (10¾-ounce) cans cream of mushroom soup
½ cup grated Cheddar cheese
Paprika

Place potatoes in the bottom of a slow cooker. Place roast over the top of the potatoes. Combine the chives with the soup, and pour over top of roast. Cover and cook on low for 8 hours. Sprinkle with cheese and paprika. Cover and cook until cheese melts. Makes 12 servings.

Chutney Ham

3 pounds boneless ham, fully cooked
1 onion, chopped
2 (6-ounce) jars mango chutney
1 tablespoon balsamic vinegar
¼ teaspoon black pepper

Place ham in a slow cooker. Mix remaining ingredients in a medium bowl, and pour over the ham. Cover and cook on low for 6 to 8 hours, until thoroughly heated. Makes 8 servings.

Corned Beef and Cabbage

1 onion, cooked and cut into wedges
4 cups hot water
2 tablespoons cider vinegar
2 tablespoons sugar
½ teaspoon black pepper
2¼ pounds whole corned-beef brisket
8 small potatoes, scrubbed and quartered
1 head green cabbage, cored and cut into wedges

Combine first 5 ingredients in a slow cooker. Mix thoroughly. Add meat and potatoes. Cover and cook on high for 4 hours. Add cabbage wedges. Cover and cook another 3 to 4 hours, or until meat is tender. Carve beef into slices, and serve with cabbage, potatoes, and sauce. Makes 8 servings.

Cranberry Pork Roast

4 potatoes, peeled and cut into 1-inch chunks
3 pounds boneless center-cut pork loin roast, rolled and tied
1 cup pearl onions
1 (16-ounce) can whole berry cranberry sauce
1 (5-ounce) can apricot nectar
½ cup coarsely chopped dried apricots
½ cup sugar
1 teaspoon dry mustard
¼ teaspoon red pepper flakes

Place the potatoes in the bottom of a slow cooker, and then place the roast over the potatoes. In a large bowl, combine the remaining ingredients; mix well and pour over roast. Cover and cook on low for 5 to 6 hours. Remove the roast to a cutting board and thinly slice. Serve with the potatoes and sauce. Makes 8 servings.

Creamy Ham and Potatoes

4 medium potatoes, sliced
2 medium onions, chopped
1½ cups cooked and cubed ham
2 tablespoons butter or margarine
2 tablespoons all-purpose flour
½ teaspoon dry mustard
½ teaspoon salt
½ teaspoon black pepper
1 (10¾-ounce) can cream of celery soup
1⅓ cups water
1 cup shredded Cheddar cheese

In a slow cooker, layer potatoes, onions, and ham. In a saucepan, melt butter. Stir in flour, mustard, salt, and pepper until smooth. Combine soup and water; gradually stir into flour mixture. Bring to a boil; cook and stir for 2 minutes until thick and bubbly. Pour over ham. Cover and cook on low for 8 to 9 hours, or until potatoes are tender. Sprinkle with cheese, cover, and allow to melt before serving. Makes 8 servings.

Curried Beef

2 pounds lean beef round, trimmed and cut into 2-inch cubes
1 garlic clove, minced
1 tablespoon curry powder
1 teaspoon cumin seeds
½ teaspoon ground cinnamon
¼ teaspoon ground ginger
½ teaspoon ground gloves
1 teaspoon allspice
1 lemon, juiced
1 tablespoon light soy sauce
1 tablespoon raisins
2 teaspoons cornstarch
¼ cup cold water

Combine ingredients, except cornstarch and cold water in a slow cooker. Cover and cook on low for 16 to 18 hours, or until meat is very tender. Gently stir meat once or twice during cooking time.

   Twenty or 30 minutes before serving time, stir the cornstarch into cold water and stir this mixture into slow cooker. Cover and continue to cook on low, stirring once or twice, until liquid thickens. Makes 8 servings.

Easiest Pork Chops

4 pork chops, well trimmed
1 (1-ounce) package onion soup mix
1 (10-ounce) can chicken broth

Brown the pork chops if you wish in a nonstick skillet, 3 to 4 minutes on each side. Place pork chops in a slow cooker. In a medium bowl, combine soup mix and chicken broth, and stir until blended. Pour this mixture over the pork chops. Cover and cook on low for 6 to 8 hours. Makes 4 servings.

French Dip Sandwich

1 (1-pound) fresh beef brisket
1 package dry onion soup mix
1 (10-ounce) can condensed beef broth

Combine all ingredients in a slow cooker. Cover and cook on low for 8 to 10 hours, until beef is tender. Skim any fat from liquid in slow cooker. Remove beef and cut across the grain into thin slices. Serve on crusty baguette rolls, and serve the hot broth for dipping. Makes 4 servings.

French Onion Beef

1¼ pounds boneless beef round steak, cut into 1-inch cubes
1 cup fresh mushrooms, sliced
1 large onion, sliced
1 (10¾-ounce) can condensed French onion soup
6 (¼-ounce) packages 15-minute stuffing mix
¼ cup margarine or butter, melted
½ cup shredded Mozzarella cheese

Place beef, mushrooms, and onion in bottom of a slow cooker. Pour soup on top. Cover and cook on low for 8 to 10 hours. Mix stuffing mix and contents of seasoning packet with melted margarine and ½ cup liquid from pot. Place stuffing in a slow cooker. Cover. Increase heat to high setting and cook for 10 minutes or until stuffing is fluffy. Sprinkle with cheese; cover. Cook until cheese is melted. Makes 8 servings.

Ham and Beans

¾ cup mixed dried beans, sorted, soaked overnight, and drained
4 cups water
¾ cup soybeans
1 cup diced carrot
1 cup diced celery
1 cup chopped onion
2 cups chopped ham
2 teaspoons salt
2 tablespoons parsley flakes
½ teaspoon thyme

Place mixed dried beans in slow cooker and cover with water. Cover and cook on low for 4 hours. Add remaining ingredients and cook 2 to 3 more hours until done. Add more water as needed. Makes 8 servings.

Ham Balls

1 pound ground beef
1½ pounds ground ham
1 pound ground pork
1 cup milk
2½ cups breadcrumbs
2 eggs, well beaten
1 cup brown sugar
1 teaspoon dry mustard
½ cup vinegar
½ cup water

Combine ground beef, ham, pork, milk, breadcrumbs, and eggs. Mix thoroughly and form into golf ball-sized balls. Place in the bottom of a slow cooker. Mix brown sugar, mustard, vinegar, and water together, and pour over meatballs. Cover and cook for 8 to 10 hours. Makes 12 servings.

Ham and Scalloped Potatoes

2 pounds ham, cut into 1-inch cubes
6 medium potatoes, peeled and thinly sliced
2 medium onions, chopped
1 (10¾-ounce) can cream of mushroom soup
2 cups shredded Colby cheese

Combine ham with potatoes and onions, and place in the bottom of a slow cooker. Pour soup over the top. Cover and cook on low for 6 to 8 hours. About an hour before serving, stir in cheese. Makes 12 servings.

Honey Barbecue Pork and Carrots

3 pounds boneless pork roast
1 (16-ounce) bag baby carrots
½ cup barbecue sauce
¼ cup honey
½ teaspoon salt
¼ teaspoon black pepper

Place pork and carrots in a slow cooker. Combine barbecue sauce, honey, salt, and pepper in a small bowl, and add to slow cooker. Cover and cook on low for 8 to 10 hours, or until pork is thoroughly cooked. Makes 8 servings.

Honey Mustard Pork Roast

2 apples, peeled and cut into 1-inch pieces
1 onion, chopped
3 tablespoons honey mustard
1 (2-pound) rolled boneless pork roast
¼ teaspoon salt
¼ teaspoon black pepper
1 tablespoon cornstarch
2 tablespoons water

In a slow cooker, mix onion and apples. Spread honey mustard over pork roast, and sprinkle with salt and pepper. Place coated roast on top of onions and apples. Cover and cook on low for 7 to 8 hours. Remove roast and cover with foil to keep warm. Combine cornstarch and water in a medium saucepan, and blend with wire whisk. Add juices, apples, and onions from the slow cooker to saucepan, and cook over medium heat until mixture boils and thickens, stirring frequently. Serve roast with sauce. Makes 8 servings.

Hungarian Goulash

1½ pounds beef stew meat
2 onions, chopped
1 clove garlic, chopped
½ cup water
1 (8-ounce) can tomato sauce
1 tablespoon paprika
2 teaspoons salt
2 teaspoons beef bouillon
¼ teaspoon black pepper
1 cup sour cream

Place all ingredients except sour cream in the bottom of a slow cooker. Cover and cook for 8 to 10 hours on low. Add sour cream to slow cooker 10 minutes before serving. Serve over noodles. Makes 4 servings.

Hungry Man

1 pound ground beef, cooked and drained
1 (16-ounce) can baked beans
¾ cup barbecue sauce
⅔ cup shredded Cheddar cheese

Combine all ingredients except cheese in a slow cooker. Cover and cook on low for 6 to 8 hours. Sprinkle with Cheddar cheese the last 15 minutes of cooking. Makes 4 servings.

Island Ribs

2½ pounds country-style pork loin ribs
¼ cup orange juice
1 tablespoon lime juice
¼ cup finely chopped onion
¼ cup barbecue sauce
1 teaspoon orange peel, grated
1 teaspoon lime peel, grated
½ teaspoon salt

Place ribs in a slow cooker. In a small bowl, combine all remaining ingredients; mix well and pour over ribs. Cover and cook on low for 7 to 9 hours. Spoon sauce over ribs to serve. Makes 8 servings.

Italian Pork Chops

6 boneless pork loin chops, well-trimmed
Salt and black pepper, to taste
1 tablespoon olive oil
1 onion, chopped
2 cups chunky pasta sauce
1 cup shredded mozzarella cheese

Sprinkle pork chops with salt and pepper. Cook chops in olive oil in a heavy skillet over medium heat until browned, about 5 minutes, turning once during cooking. Place in a slow cooker. Top with onion and pasta sauce. Cover and cook on low for 4 to 6 hours, until pork is tender and thoroughly cooked. Top with cheese just before serving. Makes 6 servings.

Italian Roast Beef

2 onions, chopped and divided
2 cloves garlic, minced
1 stalk celery, chopped
Salt and pepper, to taste
1 teaspoon dried oregano
1 teaspoon dried thyme
1 (4-pound) beef roast
½ cup all-purpose flour
1 (14½-ounce) can diced Italian-style tomatoes

In a food processor or blender, combine garlic, celery, salt, pepper, oregano, and thyme. Process to a paste. Rub roast with paste and flour and place in a slow cooker. Pour tomatoes over top. Cover and cook on low for 10 to 12 hours, or until the beef is done. Makes 12 servings.

Lamb and Veggie Curry

2 pounds lamb, cut in 1-inch cubes
3 tablespoons olive oil, divided
4 tomatoes, diced
1 tablespoon ground cumin
2 tablespoons curry powder
4 cups beef broth
1½ cups peeled and cubed butternut squash
2 cups cubed red potatoes
1 cup white pearl onions
1 pound carrots, sliced
1 cup sliced green beans
2 cups nonfat plain yogurt
Cooked rice
Coconut, chutney, raisins, peanuts, cilantro

Brown the lamb in 1½ tablespoons olive oil. Place in a slow cooker with tomatoes, cumin, and curry. Stir to distribute spices. Add enough beef broth to cover lamb, and cook on low for 6 to 8 hours. One hour prior to serving, add squash and potatoes (and more beef broth, if necessary). Fifteen minutes before serving, sauté the pearl onions, carrots, and green beans with the remaining olive oil until just tender.

Add vegetables to the slow cooker, mix thoroughly, and check the seasoning. Remove from heat and add yogurt. Serve with rice and garnishes. Makes 8 servings.

Lamb Chops with Tomatoes

1 tablespoon vegetable oil
4 loin lamb chops
2 tablespoons all-purpose flour
⅔ cup beef broth or chicken broth
1 (14½-ounce) can diced tomatoes
1 garlic clove, minced
1 tablespoon tomato paste
4 ribs celery, thinly sliced
1 teaspoon salt
Black pepper, to taste
Chopped fresh parsley

Heat oil in pan. Coat lamb chops with flour and brown quickly. Transfer chops to slow cooker. Add remaining ingredients except parsley to pan and bring to a boil. Pour over lamb, and cook on high for 30 minutes. Cover, reduce heat to low, and cook for 5 to 7 hours. Makes 4 servings.

Lamb Shanks

4 lamb shanks, well trimmed
2 garlic cloves, minced
¾ cup hot water
2 teaspoons prepared mustard
2 cubes beef bouillon
2 teaspoons prepared horseradish sauce
3 tablespoons apple or mint jelly
2 tablespoons lemon juice

Prepare broiler. Brown lamb on all sides 4 inches from heat source. Transfer lamb to a slow cooker. Add remaining ingredients and stir well. Cover and cook on low for 8 hours or on high for 4 hours. Makes 4 servings.

Marinated Lamb

1 teaspoon cornstarch
1 cup plain nonfat yogurt, stirred smooth at room temperature
2 pounds boneless lamb, cut into 2-inch pieces
1½ cups minced onions
1 cup chopped tomatoes
1½ tablespoons peeled and minced fresh ginger
1 tablespoon minced garlic
1 tablespoon ground coriander
1½ teaspoons ground cumin
¾ teaspoon cayenne pepper
¾ teaspoon turmeric
Salt, to taste
2 green chile peppers (preferably serranos), seeded and chopped
2 tablespoons vegetable oil
¼ teaspoon each of ground cinnamon, ground cardamom, ground cloves, and black pepper
Cooked rice
Chopped cilantro

Stir cornstarch into yogurt. In a large saucepan, combine yogurt, lamb, onions, tomatoes, ginger, garlic, coriander, cumin, cayenne, turmeric, salt, chiles, and vegetable oil. Mix well and let marinate 30 minutes. Cover saucepan and bring to a boil. Transfer to slow cooker, and cook on low for 5 to 7 hours, until meat is fork-tender. If too much liquid remains after meat is cooked, remove cover, raise heat, and reduce until gravy is thick.

Turn off heat, sprinkle with spices, cover, and let rest 5 minutes. Serve in bowls over rice and garnish with cilantro. Makes 8 servings.

Meatballs

1½ pounds ground beef
1 can evaporated milk
1 cup quick-cooking oatmeal
1 cup finely chopped onion
1 egg
¼ teaspoon garlic powder
¼ teaspoon salt
¼ teaspoon black pepper
1 teaspoon chili powder
1 cup ketchup
¾ cup brown sugar
¼ teaspoon garlic powder
1 teaspoon liquid smoke

Mix ground beef, evaporated milk, oatmeal, onion, and egg together. Mix in garlic powder, salt, pepper, and chili powder. Shape into walnut-sized balls. Place meatballs in bottom of a slow cooker. Mix together ketchup, brown sugar, garlic powder, and liquid smoke; pour over meatballs. Cover and cook on low for 8 hours. Makes 8 servings.

Meatloaf

1 pound lean ground beef
¼ pound pork sausage
½ cup chopped onions
½ cup chopped bell pepper
Salt and black pepper, to taste
1 tablespoon ground sage
1 teaspoon garlic powder
1 tablespoon paprika
2 eggs
¼ cup milk

Combine all ingredients and shape into a loaf. Place loaf on a trivet in the bottom of a slow cooker. Cover and cook on high for 4 hours or on low for 8 to 12 hours. Makes 6 servings.

Mexican Pork

1 pound boneless pork loin roast, cut into 1-inch pieces
1 (20-ounce) jar chunky salsa
1 (16-ounce) can pinto beans, rinsed and drained

Mix pork and salsa in a slow cooker and cover. Cook on low for 6 to 8 hours until pork is tender. Add beans, cover, and cook 10 to 15 minutes until hot. Makes 4 servings.

Mexican Ribs

4 pounds beef short ribs
1¼ cups beef stock
2½ tablespoons taco seasoning mix

Place ribs in the bottom of a slow cooker. Thoroughly mix beef stock and taco seasoning mix, and pour over the ribs. Cover and cook on low for 6 to 8 hours. Makes 8 servings.

Mushroom-Smothered Beef

½ pound fresh white mushrooms, sliced
1 medium onion, sliced
1 (10¾-ounce) can cream of mushroom soup
½ cup beef broth
2 tablespoons Worcestershire sauce, divided
1 (4-ounce) can diced green chiles
2½ pound boneless beef chuck or cross-rib roast, cut into 1½- to 2-inch cubes
3 tablespoons all-purpose flour

Combine mushrooms and onion in bottom of a slow cooker. Whisk together undiluted soup with the broth, 1 tablespoon of the Worcestershire sauce, and chiles. Pour half of soup mixture over the mushrooms and onion. Place beef on top of the mushroom mixture. Pour the remaining soup mixture on top. Do not mix. Cover and cook on low for 8 hours. Increase the heat setting to high. Mix remaining Worcestershire sauce with flour and several spoonfuls of the liquid from the slow cooker until smooth. Stir the flour mixture into the sauce in the slow cooker. Cover and cook on high for 30 minutes. Makes 5 to 6 servings.

Old-Fashioned Pot Roast

6 small potatoes
6 small onions, quartered
6 medium carrots, sliced
1 (3-pound) boneless beef chuck roast
Salt and black pepper, to taste
1 cup water

Place all ingredients in a slow cooker in the order listed. Cover and cook on low for 8 hours. Makes 8 servings.

Onion Meatballs

3 pounds frozen cooked meatballs
3 garlic cloves, minced
1 (1-ounce) package dry onion soup mix
1 (10-ounce) jar beef gravy
3 tablespoons water
⅛ teaspoon black pepper

Combine all ingredients in a slow cooker. Cover and cook on low for 4 to 5 hours until thoroughly heated. Makes 8 servings.

Pineapple Bean Pot

1 pound cooked ham, cut into ¾-inch cubes
1 onion, chopped and cooked
1 green bell pepper, chopped and cooked
2 (16-ounce) cans pinto beans, rinsed and drained
1 (16-ounce) can black beans, rinsed and drained
1 (16-ounce) can Texas-style barbecue beans, undrained
1 (20-ounce) can unsweetened pineapple chunks, drained
⅓ cup barbecue sauce
2 tablespoons prepared mustard
2 tablespoons apple cider vinegar
Black pepper, to taste

Combine first nine ingredients in a slow cooker on low heat. Mix gently. Cover and cook 5½ to 6 hours. Stir in vinegar and pepper before serving. Makes 8 servings.

Pineapple Ginger Pork

2 pounds boneless pork shoulder, trimmed and cut into 1-inch cubes
2 tablespoons cooking oil
¾ cup chicken broth
3 tablespoons quick-cooking tapioca
3 tablespoons low-sodium soy sauce
3 tablespoons oyster sauce (optional)
1 teaspoon grated fresh ginger
1 (15¼-ounce) can pineapple chunks
4 medium carrots, cut into ½-inch slices
1 large onion, cut into 1-inch pieces
1 (8-ounce) can sliced water chestnuts, drained
1½ cups fresh snow pea pods
3 cups hot cooked rice

In a large skillet, brown half of pork at a time in hot oil. Drain fat.

In a slow cooker, combine chicken broth, tapioca, soy sauce, oyster sauce, and ginger. Drain pineapple, reserving juice. Stir juice into broth mixture; cover and refrigerate pineapple chunks. Add carrots, onion, and water chestnuts to cooker. Add pork. Cover and cook on low for 6 to 8 hours or on high 3 to 4 hours.

If using a low heat setting, turn to high heat setting. Stir pineapple chunks and snow peas into cooker. Cover and cook on high for 10 to 15 minutes, or until peas are crisp-tender. Serve over rice. Makes 6 to 8 servings.

Pizza Fondue

¼ pound Italian sausage, casings removed
1 onion, cooked and chopped
1 clove garlic, minced
1 cup sliced fresh mushrooms
2 (16-ounce) cans marinara sauce
1½ cups pepperoni, chopped
1 teaspoon dried oregano
Italian bread

Sauté sausage, onion, garlic, and mushrooms in a skillet over medium-high heat until meat is browned and broken into small pieces. Drain and discard fat. Combine marinara, pepperoni, and oregano in a slow cooker. Stir in meat mixture. Cover and cook on low for 3 hours. Serve with Italian bread for dipping. Makes 8 servings.

Polish Sauerkraut and Apples

1 pound fresh or canned sauerkraut
1 pound lean smoked Polish sausage, cut into 2-inch pieces
3 tart cooking apples, cored and thickly sliced
½ cup packed brown sugar
¾ teaspoon salt
⅛ teaspoon black pepper
½ teaspoon caraway seeds (optional)
¾ cup apple juice or cider

Rinse sauerkraut and squeeze dry. Place half of the sauerkraut in a slow cooker and top with sausage. Continue to layer, in order, apples, brown sugar, salt, pepper, and, if desired, caraway seeds. Top with remaining sauerkraut. Add apple juice. Do not stir. Cover and cook on high for 3 to 3½ hours or on low for 6 to 7 hours, or until apples are tender. Stir before serving. Makes 8 servings.

Polynesian Spareribs

3 to 4 pounds pork spareribs
5 tablespoons sugar
3 tablespoons honey
3 tablespoons soy sauce
2 tablespoons ketchup
1 teaspoon seasoning salt
1 cup chicken broth

Place ribs in the bottom of a slow cooker. Mix remaining ingredients and pour over ribs. Cover and cook on low for 8 to 9 hours (if the ribs are fatty, boil them for 5 minutes before placing in the slow cooker). Makes 8 servings.

Pork Chops and Applesauce

6 boneless pork chops, browned
Salt and black pepper, to taste
¼ cup applesauce
¼ cup brown sugar
½ teaspoon ground cinnamon
1 (8-ounce) can tomato sauce
¼ cup vinegar

Sprinkle pork chops with salt and pepper to taste, and place in a slow cooker. Pour applesauce on top of the chops. Mix remaining ingredients and pour over. Cover and cook on low for 4 to 6 hours. Makes 6 servings.

Pork Fajitas

1 (2½-pound) boneless pork tenderloin, well trimmed
1 medium onion, thinly sliced
2 cups barbecue sauce
¾ cup salsa
1 tablespoon chili powder
1 teaspoon ground cumin
1 red bell pepper, seeded and chopped
1 green bell pepper, seeded and chopped
1 large onion, chopped
½ teaspoon salt
18 flour tortillas, 8 to 10 inches in diameter
Shredded cheese
Guacamole
Sour cream

Place pork in a slow cooker. Place onion slices on top. Mix barbecue sauce, salsa, chili powder, and cumin in small bowl; pour over pork and onion. Cover and cook on low 8 to 10 hours.

Remove pork, place on cutting board and shred using forks. Return to cooker and mix well. Stir in vegetables and salt. Increase heat setting to high. Cover and cook 30 minutes or until mixture is hot and vegetables are tender.

Using slotted spoon to remove pork mixture from cooker, fill each tortilla with ½ cup pork mixture. Fold tortilla into a bundle, edges down on the plate. Serve with cheese, guacamole, and sour cream. Makes 9 servings.

Pork in a Bun

1 (3- to 4-pound) pork butt, well trimmed
Salt and black pepper, to taste
2 onions, chopped
1 (16-ounce) jar prepared barbecue sauce
Buns

Season pork with salt and pepper. Place the onions in a slow cooker; place the meat on top.

Pour ½ cup barbecue sauce over the meat. Cover and cook on low for 9 to 10 hours. Remove the cooked meat from the slow cooker. Drain the juices from the pot, reserving the onions. Coarsely shred the meat into chunks, using two forks. Return the shredded meat and onions to cooker, mix in the remaining barbecue sauce, cover, and cook on low for about 1 hour. Makes 8 servings.

Pork with Fruit

2 pounds boneless pork loin roast
1½ cups mixed dried fruit
½ cup apple juice
½ teaspoon salt
¼ teaspoon black pepper

Place pork in a slow cooker, and top with fruit. Pour apple juice over pork and sprinkle with salt and pepper. Cover and cook on low for 7 to 9 hours, until pork is tender. Makes 8 servings.

Red Beans and Rice

1 pound dried red kidney beans, sorted, soaked overnight, and drained
1 cup cooked ham pieces
1 onion, chopped
1 tablespoon Worcestershire sauce
1 teaspoon hot sauce
2 bay leaves
2 garlic cloves, minced
4 tablespoons chopped parsley
4 cups water
Hot cooked rice

Place beans, ham, and seasonings in a slow cooker. Pour water over all, cover, and cook on low for 8 hours, or until beans are tender. Serve over rice. Makes 4 servings.

Roulade Steak

3 pounds thinly sliced round steaks, well trimmed
1 teaspoon salt
1 teaspoon black pepper
¾ cup chopped onion
¾ cup chopped bacon
¼ cup water
All-purpose flour

Season steaks with salt and pepper. Mix onion and bacon, and spread over steaks. Roll steaks (as you would for a jelly roll), and tie rolls tightly in several places with a string. Place steaks in a slow cooker. Add water. Cover and cook on low for 8 hours. For gravy, remove meat when done, thicken liquid with a mixture of flour and water, and cook on high for 15 minutes. Makes 8 servings.

Saucy Beef

2 pounds beef stew meat
2 (10-ounce) cans condensed tomato soup
1 (10-ounce) can condensed Cheddar cheese soup
Cooked rice or noodles

Place meat in the slow cooker; pour soups over meat, and mix well. Cover and cook 8 to 10 hours, until meat is tender. Stir well and serve over hot rice or noodles. Makes 8 servings.

Savory Short Ribs

4 pounds beef short ribs
½ teaspoon black pepper
1 (12-ounce) jar beef gravy
1 pound frozen bell peppers and onions, thawed and drained

Place ribs in a slow cooker and sprinkle with pepper. Pour gravy over top. Cover and cook on low for 9 to 11 hours, until beef is tender. Skim fat from surface of liquid and remove ribs. Cover to keep warm. Add vegetables to cooker, cover, and cook on high for 15 to 20 minutes until hot. Serve vegetables and sauce over ribs. Makes 8 servings.

Sloppy Joes

1½ pounds ground round beef
1 (16-ounce) package ground pork sausage
1 small onion, chopped
½ bell pepper, chopped
1 (8-ounce) can tomato sauce
½ cup water
½ cup ketchup
¼ cup firmly packed brown sugar
2 tablespoons cider vinegar
2 tablespoons prepared mustard
1 tablespoon chili powder
1 tablespoon Worcestershire sauce
½ teaspoon salt
¼ all-purpose flour
8 hamburger buns, toasted

Brown beef and sausage with onion and bell pepper in a large Dutch oven over medium-high heat, stirring often, for 10 minutes, or until beef and sausage crumble and are no longer pink. Drain well. Place mixture in a slow cooker. Stir in tomato sauce and next 9 ingredients. Cover and cook on high for 4 hours. Serve on hamburger buns. Makes 8 servings.

Smoked Sausage and Potatoes

2 medium onions, quartered
6 carrots, julienned
1½ cups celery, diced
1 (10½-ounce) can condensed beef broth
1 cup water
⅛ teaspoon black pepper
2 potatoes, pared and diced
2 tablespoons water
1 pound smoked sausage

Combine onions, carrots, celery, broth, water, and pepper in a slow cooker. Cover and cook for 1 hour on low. Add potatoes. Cover and cook on low for 6 hours. Add sausage and cook for an additional hour. Makes 4 servings.

Smoky Barbecue Brisket

1 (2- to 3-pound) fresh beef brisket, well trimmed
1 teaspoon chili powder
½ teaspoon garlic powder
¼ teaspoon celery seed
⅛ teaspoon black pepper
½ cup ketchup
½ cup chili sauce
¼ cup packed brown sugar
2 tablespoons vinegar
2 tablespoons Worcestershire sauce
1½ teaspoons liquid smoke
½ teaspoon dry mustard

If necessary, cut brisket to fit slow cooker. Combine chili powder, garlic powder, celery seed, and pepper; rub evenly over meat. Place meat in a slow cooker. Combine ketchup, chili sauce, brown sugar, vinegar, Worcestershire sauce, liquid smoke, and dry mustard. Pour over brisket. Cover and cook on low for 8 to 12 hours or on high for 4 to 5 hours. Makes 6 to 8 servings.

Spiced Beef Brisket

1 (4- to 5-pound) fresh beef brisket
2 cups water
1 (1-ounce) package onion soup mix
¼ cup ketchup
2 tablespoons Worcestershire sauce
½ teaspoon minced garlic
4 tablespoons all-purpose flour

Place brisket in a slow cooker. Combine water with soup mix, ketchup, Worcestershire sauce, and garlic. Pour over brisket. Cover and cook on low for 8 to 10 hours.

To make gravy, combine ¼ cup cold water and 4 tablespoons flour in a small saucepan. Stir until flour dissolves. Add ¾ cup cooking liquid. Cook and stir until bubbly. Continue cooking for an additional minute. Makes 8 to 12 servings.

Sweet and Spicy Kielbasa Sausage

1 cup brown sugar
1 tablespoon spicy mustard
2 pounds smoked kielbasa sausage, cut into 1-inch pieces

Combine brown sugar and mustard in a slow cooker; add kielbasa, and stir evenly to coat. Cover and cook on low for 2½ to 3 hours, stirring occasionally, until thoroughly heated. Makes 8 servings.

Sweet Barbecue Ribs

3½ pounds pork loin back ribs
½ teaspoon salt
¼ teaspoon black pepper
½ cup cola
⅔ cup barbecue sauce

Cut ribs into 2- or 3-rib portions, and place in slow cooker. Sprinkle with salt and pepper, and pour cola over. Cover and cook on low for 8 to 9 hours, until the ribs are tender. Drain liquid and discard. Pour barbecue sauce into a slow cooker, and mix so that ribs are coated. Cover and cook on low for 1 hour, until ribs are glazed. Makes 8 servings.

Tamale Pie

¾ cup yellow cornmeal
1 cup beef broth
1 pound extra-lean ground beef, browned and drained
1 teaspoon chili powder
½ teaspoon ground cumin (optional)
1 (14- to 16-ounce) jar thick and chunky salsa
1 (16-ounce) can whole-kernel corn, drained
¼ cup sliced olives
½ cup shredded Cheddar cheese

In a large bowl, mix cornmeal and broth; let stand 5 minutes. Stir in beef, chili powder, cumin, salsa, corn, and olives. Pour into a slow cooker. Cover and cook on low for 4 to 8 hours until set. Sprinkle cheese over top; cover and cook another 5 minutes, or until cheese melts. Makes 4 servings.

Tangy Rump Roast

1 (3- to 5-pound) rump roast, trimmed
1 (1-ounce) package onion soup mix
1 can jellied cranberry sauce
2 tablespoons butter, softened
2 tablespoons flour

Rinse rump roast and pat dry. Sprinkle onion soup mix in bottom of a slow cooker. Place rump roast in next; spoon cranberry sauce around and over roast. Cover and cook on low for 10 to 12 hours. Remove roast from slow cooker, and allow to rest while you thicken gravy. Turn slow cooker up on high. Blend softened butter and flour into a paste. Whisk it into the gravy. Cover and cook on high for about 10 minutes, until thick. Slice roast and serve with gravy. Makes 8 to 10 servings.

Tender Pork Roast

1 (3- to 4-pound) pork roast
½ cup apple juice
1 teaspoon dry mustard
1 teaspoon basil
½ teaspoon onion powder
½ cup soy sauce

Place roast in a slow cooker. Combine remaining ingredients and pour over roast. Cover and cook on low for 8 hours. Makes 6 to 8 servings.

Tender Shredded Beef

1 tablespoon olive oil
1 (2-pound) fresh beef brisket, well trimmed
1 (10-ounce) can condensed beef broth
2 garlic cloves, minced
1 onion, chopped
½ teaspoon salt
¼ teaspoon black pepper

Heat oil in 10-inch skillet over medium heat. Cook beef for 10 minutes, turning frequently, to brown all sides. Place beef in a slow cooker. Pour remaining ingredients over beef. Cover and cook on low for 8 to 10 hours, until beef is tender. Remove beef and shred using two forks. Skim fat from juices in cooker, and add beef. Keep on low setting until ready to serve. Makes 6 servings.

Teriyaki Steak

2½ pounds boneless chuck steak, cut into thin slices
1 garlic clove, crushed
2 tablespoons vegetable oil
1 teaspoon ground ginger
½ cup soy sauce
1 tablespoon brown sugar
Cooked rice

Place meat in a slow cooker. Combine remaining ingredients except rice and pour on top of steak. Cover and cook on low for 6 to 8 hours. Serve over rice. Makes 6 servings.

Viennese Pot Roast

1 onion, chopped
2 carrots, chopped
2 turnips, chopped
8 new potatoes
4 dried figs, chopped
¾ cup chicken broth
¾ cup beef broth
1 (4-pound) rump roast
4 gingersnap cookies, crushed

Place vegetables in the bottom of a slow cooker. Add the figs, chicken broth, and beef broth. Place the roast on top. Cover and cook on low for 8 to 10 hours. Set to high heat, add gingersnap cookies, and cook until thickened. Makes 8 servings.

POULTRY

Adobo Chicken

1 (3-pound) chicken, cut into pieces
1 small sweet onion, sliced
8 garlic cloves, crushed
¾ cup soy sauce
½ cup white vinegar

Place chicken in a slow cooker. Mix remaining ingredients and pour over chicken. Cover and cook on low for 6 to 8 hours. Makes 4 servings.

Almond Chicken

6 boneless, skinless chicken breasts
½ cup chicken broth
1 (10¾-ounce) can cream of mushroom [chicken] soup
½ pint sour cream
Sliced almonds

Place the chicken breasts in the bottom of a slow cooker. Mix together the broth, soup, and sour cream. Pour over the chicken. Cover and cook on low for 8 hours. Sprinkle with almonds before serving. Makes 6 servings.

Aloha Chicken

⅓ cup steak sauce
2 tablespoons honey
1 (8-ounce) can pineapple chunks, drained, reserving 2 tablespoons juice
1 medium green bell pepper, chopped
4 boneless, skinless chicken breasts

Mix steak sauce with honey and reserved pineapple juice. Place green peppers in the bottom of a slow cooker. Add chicken breasts on top. Pour honey mixture over the chicken breasts. Cover and cook on low for 4 to 6 hours. Add pineapple and cook an additional 30 to 60 minutes. Makes 4 servings.

Asian-Spiced Chicken and Beans

1 pound boneless, skinless chicken breasts, cut into ½-inch cubes
1 (16-ounce) can navy beans, drained and rinsed
1 (16-ounce) red beans, drained and rinsed
3 carrots, diagonally sliced
2½ teaspoons minced garlic
1½ teaspoons ground ginger
1¾ cups chicken broth, divided
2 tablespoons cornstarch
½ teaspoon red pepper flakes
2½ tablespoons soy sauce
4 cups cooked rice

Place chicken, beans, carrots, garlic, ginger, and 1¼ cups chicken broth in a slow cooker; stir well. Cover and cook on low for 5 hours, or until ingredients are tender.

Turn slow cooker to high. Stir in combined cornstarch and remaining chicken broth; stir in pepper. Cover and cook until thickened, about 30 minutes. Stir in soy sauce. Serve over rice. Makes 6 servings.

Barbecue Turkey Sandwich

½ cup white vinegar
½ cup ketchup
2 teaspoons Worcestershire sauce
2 teaspoons freshly ground black pepper
1 teaspoon hot pepper sauce
½ teaspoon salt
1 lemon, quartered
2 cups cooked turkey, skin removed and cut into strips or cubes
4 burger buns, split horizontally and toasted

In a slow cooker, combine vinegar, ketchup, Worcestershire sauce, pepper, hot sauce, salt, and lemon quarters. Fold in turkey, cover, and cook on high for 4 to 5 hours or on low for 8 to 9 hours. Remove lemon quarters. Serve mixture on toasted buns. Makes 4 servings.

This recipe used by permission of the National Turkey Federation.

Brown Sugar Chicken

2 pounds boneless, skinless chicken, cut into 1-inch pieces
2 tablespoons garlic, minced
2 tablespoons soy sauce
1 cup packed brown sugar
⅔ cup vinegar
¼ cup lemon-lime soda
1 teaspoon black pepper
Cooked rice

Place chicken pieces in a slow cooker. Combine remaining ingredients except rice and pour over chicken. Cover and cook on low for 6 to 8 hours. Serve with rice. Makes 4 servings.

Cheesy Chicken

6 boneless, skinless chicken breasts
1 (10¾-ounce) can cream of chicken soup
1 (10¾-ounce) can nacho cheese soup
Cooked rice or noodles

Place chicken in a slow cooker. Combine soups and pour over chicken. Cover and cook on low for 6 to 8 hours, until chicken is tender and thoroughly cooked. Serve over rice or noodles. Makes 6 servings.

Chicken and Dumplings

4 boneless, skinless chicken breasts, cut into 1-inch pieces
2 (10¾-ounce) cans cream of chicken soup
¼ cup finely diced onion
2 cups water
1 chicken bouillon cube
2 (10-ounce) packages refrigerated biscuit dough

Combine all ingredients except biscuit dough in a slow cooker. Cover and cook on low for 5 to 6 hours. Thirty minutes before serving, tear biscuit dough into 1-inch pieces. Add to the slow cooker, stirring gently. Cover and cook on high for an additional 30 minutes, or until biscuits are cooked through. Makes 8 servings.

Chicken and Shrimp

12 ounces boneless, skinless chicken thighs
1 large onion, chopped
3 garlic cloves, minced
1 (14½-ounce) can Italian-style diced tomatoes
2 tablespoons tomato paste
½ cup chicken broth
2 tablespoons lemon juice
2 bay leaves
½ teaspoon salt
¼ teaspoon red pepper flakes
½ pound frozen peeled shrimp, thawed and drained
½ pound frozen artichoke hearts, thawed and coarsely chopped
2 cups dried pasta, cooked according to package directions
½ cup crumbled feta cheese

Cut chicken thighs into quarters. Place onion and garlic in a slow cooker. Top with the chicken pieces. In a bowl, combine the undrained tomatoes, tomato paste, chicken broth, lemon juice, bay leaves, salt, and pepper. Pour over all, cover, and cook on low for 6 to 7 hours. Turn to high. Remove bay leaves. Stir in shrimp and artichoke hearts. Cover and cook for 5 minutes more. Serve chicken and shrimp mixture over hot cooked pasta. Sprinkle with feta cheese. Makes 4 servings.

Chicken and Shrimp Jambalaya

1 pound boneless, skinless chicken thighs, cut into 1-inch pieces
3 celery stalks, chopped
1 green bell pepper, chopped
2 onions, chopped
3 garlic cloves, minced
1 (28-ounce) can crushed tomatoes, undrained
1 tablespoon sugar
½ teaspoon dried oregano leaves
½ teaspoon dried basil leaves
½ cup instant rice, uncooked
1 pound frozen cooked shrimp, thawed

Combine all ingredients except rice and shrimp in a slow cooker. Cover and cook on low for 7 to 9 hours, until chicken is cooked through. Stir in rice, cover, and cook for 15 minutes, or until tender. Add shrimp, stir, cover, and cook an additional 3 to 5 minutes, or until heated through. Makes 6 servings.

Chicken Artichoke Casserole

1 (3-pound) chicken, cut into pieces
Salt and black pepper, to taste
½ teaspoon paprika
1 tablespoon butter
1 (4-ounce) can sliced mushrooms, drained
2 jars marinated artichoke hearts, drained
2 tablespoons quick-cooking tapioca
½ cup chicken broth
3 tablespoons vinegar

Season chicken with salt, pepper, and paprika. Using a large frying pan, brown chicken in butter. Place mushrooms and artichoke hearts in bottom of slow cooker. Sprinkle with tapioca. Add browned chicken pieces. Pour in broth and vinegar. Cover and cook on low for 7 to 8 hours or on high for 5 hours. Makes 8 servings.

Chicken Casserole

4 chicken thighs
4 boneless, skinless chicken breasts
Salt and black pepper, to taste
2 tablespoons butter
1 medium onion, chopped
1 (4-ounce) can sliced mushrooms, drained
½ cup chicken broth
2 teaspoons Italian seasoning
3 cups cooked rice

Season chicken with salt and pepper. In a skillet, brown chicken in butter and place in slow cooker. Sauté onion and mushrooms in skillet. Add broth to skillet and stir, scraping to remove all of the brown bits stuck to the bottom of the pan. Pour over the chicken and sprinkle with Italian seasoning. Cover and cook on high for 3 to 4 hours. Serve over rice. Makes 4 to 6 servings.

Chicken Cordon Bleu

6 boneless, skinless chicken breasts
6 pieces Swiss cheese
6 slices ham
1 (10-ounce) can condensed cream of mushroom soup with roasted garlic
3 tablespoons water
¼ teaspoon black pepper

Flatten each chicken breast with a wooden mallet or rolling pin. Place a piece of cheese and a slice of ham in the center of each. Fold up and secure with toothpicks. Place in a slow cooker. Combine remaining ingredients and pour over chicken bundles, making sure pieces are fully covered. Cover and cook on low 6 to 7 hours. Makes 6 servings.

Chicken Dinner

1 (3-pound) whole chicken
8 large carrots, peeled, cut into 2-inch pieces, and cooked
6 potatoes, peeled and sliced
1 (1-ounce) package onion soup mix
1 teaspoon dried basil
1 cup chicken broth

Place chicken, carrots, and potatoes in a slow cooker. Combine remaining ingredients and pour over. Cover and cook on high for 5 to 6 hours or on low 9 to 10 hours, until chicken leg and thigh come off easily when pulled. Makes 8 servings.

Chicken Divan

1 package frozen broccoli spears
2 to 3 boneless, skinless chicken breasts
1 (10¾-ounce) can cream of chicken soup
1¼ cups mayonnaise
1 teaspoon lemon juice

Place broccoli in the bottom of a slow cooker. Place chicken on top of broccoli. Mix together soup, mayonnaise, and lemon juice. Pour over chicken, mixing slightly. Cover and cook on low for 8 hours. Makes 2 to 3 servings.

365 Easy Slow Cooker Recipes

Chicken Marengo

1 (3-pound) whole chicken, cut into pieces
2 (1-ounce) packages spaghetti sauce mix
½ cup apple cider vinegar
½ cup chicken broth
2 fresh tomatoes, quartered
¼ pound fresh mushrooms

Place chicken parts in bottom of a slow cooker. Combine spaghetti sauce mix, vinegar, and broth; pour over chicken. Cover and cook on low for 6 to 7 hours. Add tomatoes and mushrooms. Cover and cook on high for 30 to 40 minutes, or until done. Makes 4 to 5 servings.

Chicken Spaghetti

2 pounds boneless, skinless chicken breasts or thighs
1 (1-ounce) package spaghetti sauce mix
2 garlic cloves, minced
2 onions, chopped
1 (14-ounce) can crushed tomatoes
1 (8-ounce) can tomato sauce
1 (6-ounce) can tomato paste
½ teaspoon red pepper flakes
½ teaspoon Italian seasoning
½ teaspoon black pepper
½ teaspoon ground oregano
1 (16-ounce) package dried angel hair pasta, cooked
1 cup shredded mozzarella cheese

Place chicken in a slow cooker, followed by all other ingredients except pasta and cheese. Cook on low for 6 to 8 hours. Near the end of cooking time, break up chicken into small pieces and stir. Serve over pasta and sprinkle with cheese. Makes 6 to 8 servings.

Chicken Stroganoff

1 cup light sour cream
1 tablespoon all-purpose flour
1 (1-ounce) package chicken gravy mix
1 cup water
1 pound boneless, skinless chicken breasts, cut into 1-inch pieces
1 pound bag frozen mixed vegetables, thawed and drained

In a slow cooker, mix sour cream, flour, gravy mix, and water; stir with wire whisk until well blended. Add chicken to slow cooker, stir in vegetables, cover, and cook on low for 4 hours, until chicken is tender. Cook on high for 1 hour longer, until sauce is thickened and chicken is thoroughly cooked. Makes 4 servings.

Chicken Tacos

1 (3- to 4-pound) fryer chicken, skinned if desired
1 (18-ounce) jar salsa
2 tablespoons taco seasoning mix
Taco shells

Place chicken in a slow cooker. Combine salsa and taco seasoning, and mix to blend. Pour over the chicken, cover, and cook on low for 6 to 8 hours, until chicken is tender and thoroughly cooked. Remove chicken and let cool slightly. Debone, shred meat, and stir back into cooker. Cook 20 to 30 minutes longer, until thoroughly heated. Serve in taco shells. Makes 8 servings.

Chicken Tortillas

2 pounds cooked and shredded chicken
1 (10¾-ounce) can cream of chicken soup
½ cup green chile salsa
2 tablespoons quick-cooking tapioca
12 corn tortillas
1 medium onion, chopped and divided
1½ cups grated cheese, divided
Black olives, sliced

Mix chicken with soup, salsa, and tapioca. Line bottom of a slow cooker with 3 corn tortillas, torn into pieces. Add ⅓ of the chicken mixture. Sprinkle with ⅓ of the onion and ⅓ of the grated cheese. Repeat layers of tortillas, chicken, onions, and cheese. Cover and cook on low for 6 to 8 hours. Garnish with black olives. Makes 8 servings.

Chicken Wings

5 pounds chicken wings, cut into pieces
2 cups brown sugar
½ cup prepared mustard
½ cup ketchup
¼ cup Worcestershire sauce

Put chicken in a slow cooker. Combine remaining ingredients and pour over chicken. Cook on low for 6 to 8 hours. Makes 10 servings.

Chicken with Mushrooms and Basil

1½ cups sliced fresh mushrooms
1 large onion, chopped
2 garlic cloves, minced
2½ to 3 pounds boneless, skinless chicken thighs
1 cup chicken broth
1 (6-ounce) can tomato paste
2 tablespoons quick-cooking tapioca
2 tablespoons dried basil
2 teaspoons sugar
¼ teaspoon salt
¼ teaspoon black pepper
2 cups dried noodles, cooked according to package directions
2 tablespoons grated Parmesan cheese

Combine mushrooms, onion, and garlic in a slow cooker. Place chicken on top of vegetables. Combine broth, tomato paste, tapioca, basil, sugar, salt, and pepper in a medium bowl. Pour the mixture over the chicken and vegetables.

Cover and cook on low for 7 to 8 hours or on high for 3½ to 4 hours. To serve, spoon the chicken, vegetables, and sauce over noodles. Sprinkle with cheese. Makes 4 servings.

Citrus Chicken

3 garlic cloves, minced
2 tablespoons olive oil
1 (3½-pound) whole chicken, cut up
3 bay leaves
½ cup water
1 cup orange juice
2 tablespoons lime juice
2 teaspoons black pepper
Salt, to taste

Heat garlic in olive oil. Place chicken in the bottom of a slow cooker, and add garlic and remaining ingredients. Cover and cook on low for 8 hours. Makes 8 servings.

Cola Chicken

1 (3- to 4-pound) whole chicken
1 cup ketchup
1 cup cola

Place whole chicken in a slow cooker on low heat. Combine ketchup and cola and pour over chicken. Cook on low 9 hours. Makes 8 servings.

Creamy Chicken

6 to 8 chicken pieces
1 cup evaporated milk
1 (10¾-ounce) can cream of mushroom soup
Salt and black pepper, to taste
Paprika, to taste

Place chicken in a slow cooker. Mix together evaporated milk with soup. Pour over chicken. Sprinkle with salt, pepper, and paprika. Cover and cook on low for 8 hours. Makes 6 to 8 servings.

Creamy Chicken Casserole

1½ pounds boneless, skinless chicken breasts, cut into strips
6 carrots, sliced
1 (15-ounce) can green beans
2 (10¾-ounce) cans cream of mushroom soup
2 tablespoons mayonnaise
½ cup shredded Cheddar cheese

Place chicken in bottom of a slow cooker. Mix carrots, beans, soup, and mayonnaise. Pour over chicken. Cover and cook on low for 8 to 10 hours. Sprinkle with cheese before serving. Makes 8 servings.

Creamy Italian Chicken

2 pounds boneless, skinless chicken breasts, cut into strips
¼ cup butter, melted
1 (8-ounce) container cream cheese with chives, softened
1 (10¾-ounce) can condensed golden cream of mushroom soup
1 (7-ounce) package Italian dressing mix
½ cup water
Cooked pasta or rice

Cut chicken breasts into strips and place into a slow cooker. In a medium bowl, combine butter, cream cheese, soup, Italian dressing mix, and water; stir until blended. Pour over chicken. Cover and cook on low for 6 to 8 hours. Stir well, then serve over hot cooked pasta or rice. Makes 4 to 6 servings.

Curried Chicken

4 boneless, skinless chicken breasts
½ cup honey
½ cup Dijon mustard
2 tablespoons soy sauce
¼ tablespoon curry powder

Place all ingredients in a slow cooker. Cover and cook on low for 8 hours. Makes 4 servings.

French Turkey

1½ cups dried great Northern beans, sorted, soaked overnight, and drained
1 (1-pound) turkey breast tenderloin, cut into 1-inch pieces
2 onions, chopped
1 (14-ounce) can chicken broth
1½ cups water
1 (14-ounce) can diced tomatoes, undrained
⅛ teaspoon white pepper
¼ teaspoon salt
½ teaspoon dried thyme leaves

Place beans and turkey in a slow cooker along with onions, broth, and water. Cover and cook on low for 8 to 10 hours. Stir in tomatoes and seasonings. Cover and cook on low for 30 minutes until hot. Makes 6 servings.

Garlic Pepper Chicken

4 chicken leg quarters
2 tablespoons garlic, minced
2 teaspoons black pepper
1 (10-ounce) can zucchini with tomato sauce
½ cup shredded Mozzarella cheese

Place chicken in a slow cooker. Sprinkle with garlic and pepper. Pour zucchini with tomato sauce over chicken. Cook on high for 6 hours. Sprinkle with cheese and cook until cheese melts, about 30 minutes. Makes 8 servings.

Garlic Roasted Chicken with Butter

**1 (4- to 5-pound) roasting chicken
Salt and black pepper
Paprika
4 garlic cloves, minced
½ cup butter
½ cup chicken broth**

Sprinkle chicken inside and out with salt, pepper, and paprika. Spread half of the garlic in the cavity, and spread the rest on the outside of the bird. Place bird in slow cooker, and rub a few pats of butter on its breast. Add broth and remaining butter, and cook on high for 1 hour. Reduce to low and cook for 5 to 7 hours longer, until tender and juices run clear. Serve garlic butter sauce with chicken. Makes 8 to 10 servings.

Herbed Turkey Cutlets

2 pounds turkey cutlets, cut into ⅓-pound portions
½ teaspoon salt
½ teaspoon black pepper
2 tablespoons unsalted butter
1 medium onion, thinly sliced
½ cup sliced button mushrooms
½ cup chicken broth
½ teaspoon dried oregano
½ teaspoon dried thyme
Cooked rice

Sprinkle turkey with salt and pepper. Over medium-high heat, melt butter in a hot skillet. Add turkey and quickly brown both sides. With a slotted spoon, transfer cutlets to slow cooker. Sauté onion and mushrooms in hot skillet until vegetables are soft. Reduce heat and add broth. Simmer for 10 to 15 minutes. Pour mixture over turkey. Sprinkle with herbs. Cover and cook on low setting for 6 to 8 hours or on high setting for 2½ to 3 hours. Serve over rice with juice from the pot. Makes 6 servings.

This recipe used by permission of the National Turkey Federation.

Home-Style Turkey Dinner

3 medium Yukon gold potatoes, cut into 2-inch pieces
3 pounds turkey thighs, skin removed
1 (12-ounce) jar home-style turkey gravy
2 tablespoons all-purpose flour
1 teaspoon dried parsley
½ teaspoon dried thyme
⅛ teaspoon freshly ground black pepper
1 (16-ounce) bag frozen baby green bean and carrot blend, thawed and drained
Fresh thyme sprigs, for garnish
1 cup cranberry sauce

Place potatoes in a slow cooker. Arrange turkey thighs on top of potatoes. In a medium bowl, mix gravy, flour, herbs, and pepper until smooth. Pour mixture over turkey. Cover and cook on low for 8 to 10 hours, or until the internal temperature reaches 180°. Stir in vegetables and continue to cook covered on low for 30 more minutes or until vegetables are tender. Using a slotted spoon, remove turkey and vegetables from the slow cooker. Garnish turkey with fresh thyme and serve with juices or cranberry sauce. Makes 8 servings.

This recipe used by permission of the National Turkey Federation.

Honey Hoisin Chicken

2 tablespoons soy sauce
2 tablespoons hoisin sauce
2 tablespoons honey
2 tablespoons chicken broth
1 tablespoon grated fresh ginger
¼ teaspoon salt
⅛ teaspoon black pepper
2½ to 3 pounds chicken pieces
2 tablespoons cornstarch
2 tablespoons cold water
Sesame seeds, toasted

Combine soy sauce, hoisin sauce, honey, broth, ginger, salt, and pepper. Dip each piece of chicken into sauce; place in a slow cooker. Pour remaining sauce over chicken. Cover and cook on low about 4 to 5 hours, or until chicken is tender.

    Remove chicken from slow cooker and keep warm. Dissolve cornstarch in cold water. Stir mixture into juices. Cover and cook on high 15 to 20 minutes, or until slightly thickened. To serve, spoon sauce over chicken and sprinkle with sesame seeds. Makes 8 servings.

Hunter's Turkey

1 large green bell pepper, chopped
1 cup sliced sweet onions
2 celery stalks, chopped into ¼-inch slices
1 cup sliced fresh mushrooms
2 pounds turkey cutlets, cut into 4-ounce portions
⅛ teaspoon garlic salt
½ teaspoon black pepper
¼ teaspoon ground cinnamon
¼ cup chicken broth
1 (15-ounce) can crushed tomatoes
3 tablespoons all-purpose flour
3 tablespoons cold water
Cooked pasta

Place vegetables in slow cooker set on low. Sprinkle both sides of each turkey cutlet with garlic salt, pepper, and cinnamon. Layer cutlets atop vegetables. Add broth and tomatoes. Stir well to combine all ingredients. Cover and cook on low for 7 to 10 hours or on high for 2 to 3 hours. Make a smooth paste of flour and water. Stir into ingredients, blending well. Cover and cook on high for 20 to 25 minutes, or until the sauce has thickened. Serve over cooked pasta. Makes 8 servings.

This recipe used by permission of the National Turkey Federation.

Island Chicken

1 (8-ounce) can pineapple chunks in heavy syrup
2 pounds chicken thighs and breasts
1 (10¾-ounce) can chicken broth
¼ cup vinegar
2 tablespoons brown sugar
2 teaspoons soy sauce
1 garlic clove, minced
1 green bell pepper, cut into 1-inch pieces
3 tablespoons cornstarch
¼ cup water

Drain pineapple and reserve liquid. Put chicken parts in bottom of a slow cooker. Mix together pineapple syrup, chicken broth, vinegar, brown sugar, and soy sauce in a saucepan. Heat until brown sugar dissolves. Pour over chicken. Cover and cook on high for 1 hour. Add pineapple chunks, garlic, and bell pepper. Cover and cook on low for 7 to 9 hours. Half an hour before serving, mix together cornstarch and water, and add to the slow cooker to thicken. Makes 8 servings.

Italian Chicken

1½ pounds boneless, skinless chicken breasts
4 garlic cloves, minced
2 potatoes, cubed
½ cup zesty Italian salad dressing
⅛ teaspoon black pepper

Combine all ingredients in a slow cooker. Cover and cook on low for 6 to 8 hours, or until chicken is thoroughly cooked and potatoes are tender. Makes 4 servings.

Italian Turkey Sandwiches

1 pound Italian turkey sausage, casings removed
1½ pounds ground turkey
1 large sweet onion, thinly sliced
2 large green bell peppers, chopped
2 large red bell peppers, chopped
1 teaspoon salt
1 teaspoon black pepper
¼ teaspoon red pepper flakes
10 hoagie rolls
1¼ pounds grated provolone cheese

Over medium heat, brown sausage and ground turkey, breaking up into medium pieces. Cook until sausage is no longer pink. Remove from skillet with a slotted spoon and reserve.

In a bowl, toss vegetables together with salt, pepper, and red pepper flakes. Place one-third of the vegetable mixture in a slow cooker. Layer one-half of the turkey mixture atop the vegetables. Repeat layers of raw vegetables and browned turkey, ending with a top layer of vegetables. Cover and cook on low for 6 hours, or until the vegetables are tender. Serve on split rolls. Sprinkle each sandwich with cheese. Makes 10 servings.

This recipe used by permission of the National Turkey Federation.

Jamaican Chicken Curry

1 medium onion, diced
1 orange or red bell pepper, cut into 1-inch pieces
1 tablespoon canola oil
3 garlic cloves, minced
2 tablespoons fresh ginger, minced
2 teaspoons curry powder
1 teaspoon ground allspice
1 teaspoon ground cumin
4 boneless, skinless chicken breasts, cut into 1-inch cubes
2 cups chicken stock
Salt and pepper, to taste
Cooked rice

Cook onion and pepper in oil until onion softens. Add garlic and ginger and cook until fragrant. Add spices and stir for 1 minute. Put vegetable mixture into slow cooker.

    Add raw chicken on top. Pour chicken stock over all, stir, cover, and cook on low for 5 to 6 hours. Season to taste, and serve with rice. Makes 6 servings.

Kona Chicken

3 pounds boneless, skinless chicken breast, cut into 1-inch cubes
½ cup chopped green onions
½ cup soy sauce
¼ cup chicken broth
½ cup water
½ cup honey

Place chicken in a slow cooker. Mix together onions, soy sauce, chicken broth, and water. Pour over top of chicken. Cover and cook on low for 3 to 5 hours, until chicken is tender. Remove chicken from slow cooker. Brush with honey and place in broiler. Broil until golden brown, brushing with honey several times. Serve with sauce from slow cooker. Makes 8 servings.

Lacquered Chicken

1 tablespoon vegetable oil
1 (2-pound) whole chicken
3 very large onions, peeled and chopped
5 large tomatoes, chopped
1 medium orange, peeled, seeded, and chopped
1 teaspoon sugar
1 teaspoon salt
⅛ teaspoon black pepper
½ cup water
1 chicken bouillon cube, crumbled
3 tablespoons red currant, raspberry, or red grape jelly
¼ cup apple cider

Heat the oil in a skillet, and sauté the chicken, turning often, until well browned. Remove and set aside. Sauté onion in skillet until well browned. Put onions in the bottom of a slow cooker. Place tomatoes, orange, sugar, salt, and pepper in the pot, and set chicken on top. Add the water and bouillon cube. Cover and cook on low for 5 to 7 hours.

Before serving, remove the chicken to a deep serving dish and keep warm. Place the vegetables from the slow cooker in a skillet, and simmer until thick. Stir in jelly and apple cider, and cook, stirring until the sauce boils. Do not overcook, lest the sauce lose its shiny quality. If sauce is not shiny enough, bring back to a very brisk boil and quickly stir in some jelly. Pour sauce over the chicken. Makes 8 servings.

Lemon Chicken

2 boneless, skinless chicken breasts
Juice of half of a lemon
Salt and black pepper, to taste

Place chicken in a slow cooker. Squeeze lemon juice over the chicken. Sprinkle with salt and pepper. Cover and cook on low for 6 to 8 hours. Add more lemon juice if needed. Makes 2 servings.

Lemon Pepper Chicken

4 boneless, skinless chicken breasts
Lemon pepper seasoning
2 teaspoons butter, melted

Sprinkle chicken breasts with lemon pepper seasoning to taste. Place chicken in a slow cooker. Pour butter over top of chicken. Cover and cook on low for 8 to 10 hours. Makes 4 servings.

Lime Chicken

4 boneless, skinless chicken breasts
¼ cup lime juice
2 tablespoons olive oil
½ teaspoon dried oregano
½ teaspoon garlic salt

Combine all ingredients in a slow cooker. Cover and cook on low for 8 hours. Add water if necessary. Makes 4 servings.

Maple-Glazed Turkey Breast

1 (6-ounce) package long grain wild rice mix
1¼ cups water
2 pounds boneless turkey breast, thawed if frozen
1 onion, chopped
¼ cup maple syrup
¼ teaspoon ground cinnamon
½ teaspoon salt
⅛ teaspoon white pepper

Combine rice, its seasoning mix packet, and water in a slow cooker. Place turkey breast on top, sprinkle with onions, and drizzle with maple syrup. Sprinkle with cinnamon, salt, and pepper. Cover and cook on low for 5 to 6 hours, or until turkey is thoroughly cooked and registers 180° on a meat thermometer. Makes 4 servings.

Mexican Turkey

2 dried ancho chiles
2 cups boiling water
1 tablespoon vegetable oil
2½ pounds turkey breast, skin on
2 medium onions, sliced
3 garlic cloves, sliced
2 serrano chiles, chopped
4 whole cloves
1 tablespoon chili powder
¼ teaspoon ground cinnamon
1 teaspoon salt
1 teaspoon black peppercorns, crushed
1 (28-ounce) can tomatillos, drained
½ cup whole blanched almonds
1 ounce unsweetened chocolate, broken into pieces
¼ cup finely chopped cilantro
3 tablespoons diced mild green chiles

In a heat-proof bowl, soak dried ancho chiles in boiling water for 30 minutes, making sure all parts of the pepper are submerged. Drain and discard water. Coarsely chop chili and set aside.

In a skillet, heat oil over medium-high heat. Add turkey breast and brown on both sides. Transfer to slow cooker.

Reduce skillet temperature to medium heat. Add onions to pan and cook, stirring, until softened. Stir in ancho chiles, garlic, serrano chiles, cloves, chili powder, cinnamon, salt, and pepper. Cook, stirring, for 1 minute. Transfer mixture to a food processor. Add tomatillos, almonds, and chocolate, and process until smooth. Pour sauce over turkey, cover, and cook on high for 4 hours or on low for 8 hours, or until the internal temperature of the turkey reaches 180°. Garnish with cilantro and chiles. Makes 8 servings.

This recipe used by permission of the National Turkey Federation.

Onion and Mushroom Chicken

2½ to 3 pounds chicken, cut up
1 can pearl onions, drained
1 garlic clove, minced
1 (1-ounce) package onion mushroom soup
½ teaspoon salt
¼ teaspoon thyme
1½ cups beef broth
½ cup water
2 tablespoons chopped fresh parsley

Place the chicken, onion, and garlic in a slow cooker. Mix remaining ingredients and pour over chicken. Cover and cook on low for 8 hours. Makes 6 to 8 servings.

Orange Chicken

½ teaspoon salt
½ teaspoon paprika
4 boneless, skinless chicken breasts
1 cup chopped onion
½ cup chopped bell pepper
½ cup chopped celery
2 garlic minced cloves
¾ cup orange juice
1 teaspoon grated orange peel
2 tablespoons honey
1 tablespoon Worcestershire sauce
½ teaspoon ground ginger

Sprinkle salt and paprika over chicken. Set aside. Place onion, bell pepper, celery, and garlic in the bottom of a slow cooker. Place chicken on top. Mix orange juice, peel, honey, Worcestershire sauce, and ginger. Pour over chicken. Cover and cook on low for 6 to 8 hours. Makes 4 servings.

Orange-Glazed Chicken

½ cup orange marmalade
⅓ cup bottled Russian dressing
½ (1-ounce) package onion soup mix
6 frozen boneless, skinless chicken breasts, unthawed

Mix the first three ingredients together. Place chicken in a slow cooker and cover with marmalade mixture. Cover and cook on low for 6 to 8 hours. Makes 6 servings.

Peachy Chicken

4 boneless, skinless chicken thighs
2 sweet potatoes, peeled and cubed
1 onion, chopped
2 tablespoons water
3 tablespoons cornstarch
½ cup peach preserves

Place chicken in a slow cooker, and top with sweet potatoes and onion. Cover and cook on low for 7 to 8 hours, until chicken is thoroughly cooked and sweet potatoes are tender. Remove chicken and vegetables from slow cooker with a slotted spoon, and cover with foil to keep warm.

In a heavy saucepan, combine water and cornstarch and mix well. Add juices from slow cooker along with preserves. Cook over medium heat, stirring frequently, until mixture boils and thickens. Cook for 2 minutes, and pour over chicken and vegetables. Makes 4 servings.

Peanut Chicken

3½ pounds boneless, skinless chicken breasts
⅓ cup peanut butter
2 tablespoons low-sodium soy sauce
3 tablespoons orange juice
⅛ teaspoon black pepper
Cooked rice or noodles

Combine all ingredients in a slow cooker; mix well. Cover and cook on low for 6 to 8 hours, or until chicken is thoroughly cooked. Serve over rice or noodles. Makes 8 servings.

Pizza Chicken

8 boneless, skinless chicken breasts
¼ teaspoon salt
⅛ teaspoon black pepper
1 onion, chopped
2 bell peppers, cut into 1-inch pieces
2 cups pasta sauce
1 cup shredded mozzarella cheese
Cooked pasta or rice

Sprinkle chicken with salt and pepper, and place in a slow cooker. Top with onions and bell peppers, and pour pasta sauce over all. Cover and cook on low 6 to 8 hours, or until chicken is thoroughly cooked. Stir well, then sprinkle with cheese, and let stand 5 minutes to melt cheese. Serve over pasta or rice. Makes 8 servings.

Pulled Chicken

4 boneless, skinless chicken breasts
6 ounces barbecue sauce
1 (12-ounce) can cola (optional)

Place chicken, barbecue sauce, and cola in slow cooker. Cook on low for 8 hours. Shred cooked chicken with fork. Makes 4 to 6 servings.

Roasted Chicken

1 (6-ounce) package cornbread dressing
1¼ cups water
¼ cup chicken broth
12 carrots, peeled and cut into 2-inch pieces
1 (4- to 5-pound) roasting chicken
Salt and black pepper, to taste

Prepare dressing according to package's directions with 1¼ cups water. Set aside to cool. When cool, stir in broth. Meanwhile, in saucepan, cook carrots in small amount of water for 5 minutes. Drain and place in slow cooker. Rinse and dry chicken; stuff with dressing. Place on top of carrots in slow cooker. Sprinkle with salt and pepper. Cover and cook on low for 6 to 8 hours, or until chicken is tender. Makes 6 to 7 servings.

Smothered Chicken and Vegetables

3 carrots, sliced
3 celery stalks, sliced
1 large onion, cut into thin wedges
1 pound cooked and cubed chicken
1 (10¾-ounce) can condensed cream of celery soup
¾ cup chicken broth

Place vegetables in the bottom of a slow cooker. Top with chicken. Add soup and broth. Cover and cook for 4 to 6 hours on low. Makes 4 servings.

Sour Cream and Bacon Chicken

8 bacon slices
8 boneless, skinless chicken breasts
2 (10¾-ounce) cans roasted garlic cream of mushroom soup
1 cup sour cream
½ cup flour

Wrap one slice of bacon around each boneless chicken breast and place in a slow cooker. In a medium bowl, combine soup, sour cream, and flour, and mix with wire whisk to blend. Pour over chicken. Cover and cook on low for 6 to 8 hours, or until chicken and bacon are thoroughly cooked. Makes 8 servings.

South of the Border Chicken

4 boneless, skinless chicken breasts
1 (10¾-ounce) can broccoli cheese soup
⅓ cup evaporated milk
4 cups hot cooked rice
Salsa
Sour cream
1 small avocado, sliced (optional)

Place chicken in the bottom of a slow cooker. Combine soup and milk; pour over chicken. Cover and cook on low for 7 to 8 hours. Serve with rice. Top with salsa, sour cream, and avocado. Makes 4 servings.

Southwest Turkey Loaf

⅔ cup salsa
1 egg, beaten
¼ teaspoon black pepper
¼ teaspoon salt
1¼ pounds ground turkey

In a medium bowl, combine salsa, egg, pepper, and salt, and mix well. Add ground turkey and combine. Form into a 6-inch round loaf, and place on a rack in a slow cooker. Cover and cook on low for 4 to 5 hours, until turkey is thoroughly cooked. Makes 4 servings.

Soy Chicken

½ cup vinegar
2½ tablespoons soy sauce
6 to 8 garlic cloves, crushed
½ teaspoon black peppercorns
1 bay leaf
½ tablespoon salt
1 (3 to 4-pound) chicken, cut into serving-sized portions
¼ cup water

In a slow cooker, combine liquids and seasonings. Add chicken. Cover and cook on high for 1 hour. Add water. Cover and cook on low for 4 to 5 hours. Makes 6 to 8 servings.

Spicy Chicken

1 (3-pound) whole chicken
1 medium potato, peeled and sliced
2 onions, finely chopped
4 to 7 garlic cloves, minced
2 bay leaves
1 teaspoon ground cumin
1 teaspoon dried oregano
1 tablespoon chili powder
2 cups soft white breadcrumbs
2 chicken bouillon cubes
1¾ cups water
Fresh cilantro, chopped

Place chicken in a slow cooker. Place potato slices around bottom sides of cooker. Add onions, garlic, spices, and breadcrumbs, pushing the crumbs down around the chicken. Microwave bouillon cubes with water and pour over the chicken. Cover and cook on low heat 7 hours or high heat for 4 hours.

    Remove lid and let cool for about 20 minutes. Carefully lift chicken onto a plate, using two wide-slotted spoons. Remove bay leaves, skin, and bones. When sauce in cooker has cooled slightly, strain into a food processor or blender, and process until smooth. Serve chicken with sauce, and garnish with cilantro. Makes 8 servings.

Sunshine Chicken

8 boneless, skinless chicken breasts
1 cup barbecue sauce
1 cup orange juice

Place chicken in a slow cooker. Combine liquids and pour over chicken. Cover and cook on low for 8 hours. Makes 8 servings.

Sweet-and-Sour Chicken

4 to 5 pounds chicken thighs, legs, and breasts
2 tablespoons apple cider vinegar
1 tablespoon soy sauce
2 tablespoons oil
⅓ cup water
½ cube chicken bouillon
1 tablespoon brown sugar
1 teaspoon thyme
½ teaspoon salt
Dash black pepper
2 garlic cloves, crushed
2 tablespoons chopped fresh parsley

Place chicken in the bottom of a slow cooker. Mix remaining ingredients and pour over chicken. Cover and cook on low for 8 to 10 hours. Makes 8 to 10 servings.

Tangy Chicken Thighs

2 pounds boneless, skinless chicken thighs, cut into 1½-inch pieces
1 (14-ounce) diced can tomatoes, undrained
1 (6-ounce) can tomato paste
1 onion, chopped
2 garlic cloves, crushed
2 cups diced carrots
1 tablespoon dried basil
1 teaspoon dried oregano
½ teaspoon dried thyme, crushed
½ teaspoon rosemary, crumbled
½ teaspoon black pepper
½ cup fresh orange juice
1½ teaspoons sugar
2 tablespoons orange zest, divided
2 tablespoons lemon juice
4 slices cooked bacon, crumbled

Combine chicken, tomatoes, tomato paste, onion, garlic, carrots, basil, oregano, thyme, rosemary, pepper, orange juice, sugar, and 1 tablespoon orange zest in a slow cooker. Mix thoroughly. Cover and cook on low for 6 to 6½ hours, or until chicken is cooked throughout. Stir in lemon juice and remaining orange zest. Serve sprinkled with crumbled bacon. Makes 6 servings.

Taverna Chicken

1 (4-pound) chicken, cut into serving-sized portions
1 onion, chopped
2 garlic cloves, minced
1 green bell pepper, chopped
1 medium ripe tomato, peeled and chopped
1 cup chicken broth
Dash cayenne pepper

Combine all ingredients in a slow cooker. Cover and cook on low for 6 to 8 hours. Makes 8 servings.

Tennessee Chicken Breasts

4 boneless, skinless chicken breasts
¼ cup all-purpose flour
½ teaspoon paprika
Salt and black pepper, to taste
2 tablespoons butter
2 tablespoons oil
2 tablespoons chopped onion
2 tablespoons chopped fresh parsley
¼ teaspoon dried chervil
¼ cup chicken broth
1 (4-ounce) can sliced mushrooms, undrained
1 (10-ounce) can tomatoes
¼ teaspoon sugar
Cooked noodles or rice

Dredge chicken in flour that has been mixed with paprika and a little salt and pepper. Heat butter and oil in a skillet, and sauté chicken on both sides until lightly browned. Stir in onion, parsley, and chervil, and cook briefly. Remove from heat. Place chicken in a slow cooker. Combine remaining ingredients except noodles, and pour over chicken. Cover and cook on low for 6 to 8 hours. Serve with noodles or rice. Makes 4 servings.

Three-Ingredient Turkey

1 (3- to 4-pound) frozen turkey breast, thawed
1 (16-ounce) can cranberry sauce
1 (1-ounce) package onion soup mix

Place ingredients in a slow cooker, cover, and cook on high for 2 hours. Then reduce heat to low, and continue cooking for 4 to 5 hours, until turkey registers 180° on an instant meat thermometer. Slice turkey breast and serve with sauce. Makes 8 servings.

Turkey Breast

1 (2- to 3½-pound) frozen turkey breast, thawed
½ cup orange juice
½ cup water
⅛ cup sugar
1 teaspoon dried rosemary
½ teaspoon dried thyme

Place frozen turkey breast in a slow cooker. Pour remaining ingredients on top. Cover and cook on low for 7 to 8 hours. Makes 8 servings.

Turkey Breast with Marmalade Sauce

1 (2- to 3½-pound) frozen turkey breast, thawed
1 jar orange marmalade
Ground cinnamon

Place turkey breast in a slow cooker, pour marmalade over top, and sprinkle with cinnamon. Cover and cook on low for 6 to 8 hours. Makes 8 servings.

Turkey Dijon

1 fresh bone-in turkey breast
3 tablespoons Dijon mustard
1 teaspoon salt
⅛ teaspoon black pepper
⅔ cup 100% fruit juice

Put turkey breast, skin side up, in a slow cooker. Spread with Dijon mustard and season with salt and pepper . Pour juice over the turkey, cover, and cook on low for 8 to 9 hours, until turkey is tender and thoroughly cooked. Makes 8 servings.

Turkey Nachos

3 pounds boneless, skinless turkey thighs
1 (1¼-ounce) package taco seasoning mix
1 (14½-ounce) can diced tomatoes, with juices
1 (15-ounce) can pinto beans
1 (4½-ounce) can chopped green chiles
1 teaspoon dried oregano
½ teaspoon ground cumin
2 tablespoons fresh lime juice
White corn tortilla chips
1 cup shredded jalapeño cheese
1 cup finely chopped red bell pepper
¼ cup black olives, well drained
¼ cup chopped green onions
⅔ cup sour cream
¼ cup fresh cilantro sprigs
⅔ cup salsa
10 lime wedges, seeds removed

Place thighs in a slow cooker and sprinkle with taco seasoning. Cover with tomatoes, beans, chiles, oregano, cumin, and lime juice. Cover and cook on low for 7 to 8 hours.

Remove turkey thighs from cooker, and allow to slightly cool. Shred into thin strips. Mash beans with tomatoes, chiles, and herbs. Return turkey to cooker and blend all together. Continue to heat on low for up to 2 hours.

Place chips on large oven-proof platter. Spoon turkey mixture onto chips. Sprinkle with cheese, bell pepper, olives, and onions. Heat at 425° for about 5 minutes, or until cheese melts. Serve with sour cream, cilantro, salsa, and lime. Makes 8 servings.

This recipe used by permission of the National Turkey Federation.

Turkey Parmesan Meatballs

1½ pounds ground turkey
¼ cup pesto sauce
1 teaspoon red pepper flakes
⅓ cup grated Parmesan cheese
1 sweet onion, minced
½ teaspoon salt
2 teaspoons vegetable oil
2 (28-ounce) cans diced tomatoes
1 tablespoon pesto sauce
1 (6-ounce) can tomato paste
1 teaspoon granulated sugar
¼ cup beef broth
Cooked pasta

In a large bowl, combine ground turkey, ¼ cup pesto, red pepper flakes, Parmesan cheese, onion, and salt. Shape mixture into two dozen 1½-inch balls. In a large nonstick skillet, heat oil. Place meatballs in skillet, cook 1 to 2 minutes per side, until lightly browned.

Place meatballs in slow cooker. Add diced tomatoes, pesto sauce, tomato paste, sugar, and beef broth. Stir carefully to combine. Cook on high for 4 to 6 hours, or until meatballs are cooked through. Serve over pasta. Makes 12 servings.

Turkey Roast with Vegetables

1 cup chopped onion
3 cups diced red potato
1 pound fresh baby carrots
1 (10¾-ounce) can cream of celery soup
½ cup cold water
1 teaspoon poultry seasoning
¼ teaspoon salt
3 pounds boneless turkey breast roast, thawed if frozen
1 tablespoon no-salt seasoning blend
¼ cup instant mashed potato flakes
Fresh parsley leaves, chopped fine

Coat a slow cooker with nonstick cooking spray. Place onion, potato, and carrots in slow cooker. Stir together soup, water, poultry seasoning, and salt. Pour over vegetables. Pat turkey breast roast dry with clean paper towels. Lift string netting, and shift position on roast for easier removal after cooking. Sprinkle seasoning blend over roast, and place roast on vegetables. Cover and cook on low for 6 to 8 hours, or until the internal temperature registers 180°. Remove roast from slow cooker. Let stand 10 minutes. Meanwhile, stir potato flakes and parsley into vegetables. Let stand 5 minutes. Remove string netting, cut roast into slices, and serve with vegetables. Makes 8 servings.

This recipe used by permission of the National Turkey Federation.

Turkey Sandwiches

6 cups cooked and diced turkey
3 cups diced cheese
1 (10¾-ounce) can cream of mushroom soup
1 (10¾-ounce) can cream of chicken soup
1 onion, chopped
½ cup mayonnaise
8 hoagie rolls

Combine all ingredients except rolls in a slow cooker. Cook on high for 3 to 4 hours or on low for 6 to 8 hours. Stir occasionally. Add a bit of broth, milk, or water if mixture becomes too thick. Serve on hoagie rolls. Makes 8 servings.

Turkey Stuffing

1 cup butter
2 cups chopped onion
2 cups chopped celery
¼ cup chopped fresh parsley
2 (8-ounce) cans sliced mushrooms
12 cups day-old bread cubes
1 teaspoon poultry seasoning
1½ teaspoons sage
1 teaspoon thyme
½ teaspoon black pepper
¼ teaspoon garlic powder
3½ cups chicken or turkey broth
2 eggs, well beaten

Melt butter in a skillet, and sauté onion, celery, parsley, and mushrooms. Pour over bread cubes in a very large mixing bowl. Add all seasonings and toss well. Pour in enough broth to moisten. Add eggs and mix well. Pack lightly into a slow cooker. Cover and cook on low 6 to 8 hours. Makes 12 servings.

Turkey Teriyaki Sandwich

1½ pounds boneless, skinless turkey thighs
½ cup teriyaki baste and glaze sauce
3 tablespoons orange marmalade
¼ teaspoon black pepper
8 hoagie buns

Combine all ingredients except buns in a slow cooker; cover and cook on low for 9 to 10 hours. Remove turkey from slow cooker, shred using two forks, and return to cooker. Cook on high for 10 to 15 minutes, until sauce is thickened. Serve on hoagie buns. Makes 8 servings.

Wild Duck

2 ducks
2 cups beef stock
1 onion, chopped
1 carrot, diced
¼ bell pepper, diced
1 (4-ounce) can sliced mushrooms
Salt and black pepper, to taste
1 cup instant rice

Place all ingredients except rice in slow cooker and cook on low for 8 to 10 hours. Remove duck from slow cooker and debone. Turn cooker to high for 30 minutes, or until boiling. Return duck to cooker with 1 cup rice; cook until rice is done. Makes 6 to 8 servings.

Wild Rice-Stuffed Turkey

1½ cups wild rice, rinsed
1 onion, finely chopped
½ cup dried cranberries
2 apples, cored and chopped
3 cups water
4 to 5 pounds boneless whole turkey breast, thawed if frozen

Mix rice, onion, dried cranberries, and apples; place in bottom of a slow cooker. Pour water over, making sure all wild rice is submerged. Place turkey on top of rice mixture.

Cover and cook on low for 8 to 9 hours, or until turkey is thoroughly cooked and reaches 180° on a meat thermometer, and wild rice is tender. Makes 10 servings.

SEAFOOD

Baked Salmon

2 (16-ounce) cans salmon
1 green bell pepper, chopped
4 cups breadcrumbs
2 chicken bouillon cubes, dissolved in 1 cup boiling water
1 teaspoon fresh lemon juice
1 cup boiling water
4 eggs, well beaten
1 teaspoon garlic powder
1 teaspoon Greek seasoning
¼ teaspoon dry mustard
1 teaspoon dill weed, finely chopped

In a well-greased slow cooker, combine all of the ingredients. Cover and cook on high for 4 to 5 hours. Makes 4 servings.

Bouillabaisse

2 pounds boneless fish fillets, cut into 1-inch cubes
1 pound shrimp, peeled and deveined
1½ pounds scallops
2 cups shucked clams
1 cup chopped onion
1 cup chopped celery
2 (16-ounce) cans tomatoes
1 cup vegetable broth
½ cup olive oil

Place all ingredients in a slow cooker; stir to blend. Cover and cook on low for 3 to 4 hours. Makes 6 to 8 servings.

Caribbean Shrimp

1 pound shrimp, peeled and deveined
1 teaspoon orange zest
¼ cup orange juice
¼ cup lime juice
1 teaspoon brown sugar
2 garlic cloves, minced
1 teaspoon chili powder
½ teaspoon dried oregano
1 teaspoon salt
1 cup frozen peas
1 tomato, diced
Cooked rice

In a slow cooker, combine the shrimp, orange zest, juices, brown sugar, garlic, chili powder, oregano, and salt. Cover and cook on low for 2 hours. Stir in peas and tomatoes, increase heat to high, and cook covered for 10 more minutes. Serve over rice. Makes 4 servings.

Caribbean Shrimp and Rice

1 (12-ounce) package frozen shrimp, thawed
½ cup chicken broth
½ teaspoon garlic powder
1 teaspoon chili powder
½ teaspoon dried oregano
Salt, to taste
1 cup frozen peas
½ cup diced tomatoes
2 cups cooked rice

Combine shrimp, broth, and dry seasonings in slow cooker. Cover and cook on low for 2 hours. Add peas, tomatoes, and rice. Cover and cook on high for 10 minutes, or until heated through. Makes 2 servings.

Chow Mein Casserole

1 small green bell pepper, chopped
1 cup chopped celery
¼ cup chopped onion
1 (7-ounce) can tuna fish, drained
1 (10¾-ounce) can cream of mushroom soup
¼ cup milk
1 cup chow mein noodles

Mix all ingredients except chow mein noodles in a slow cooker. Cover and cook on low for 7 to 8 hours. Add chow mein noodles during the last hour of cooking. Makes 2 servings.

Coconut Thai Shrimp and Rice

2 (10-ounce) cans chicken broth
1 cup water
1 teaspoon ground coriander
½ teaspoon ground cumin
1 teaspoon salt
½ teaspoon cayenne pepper
2 limes, zest and juice only
7 garlic cloves, minced
1 tablespoon minced fresh ginger
1 medium onion, chopped
1 red bell pepper, chopped
1 carrot, peeled and shredded
¼ cup flaked coconut
½ cup golden raisins
2 cups instant rice
1 pound jumbo shrimp, peeled and deveined
½ cup fresh snow peas, cut into strips
Toasted coconut for garnish, optional

In a slow cooker, combine chicken broth, water, coriander, cumin, salt, cayenne pepper, lime zest, lime juice, garlic, and ginger. Stir in onion, pepper, carrot, coconut, raisins, and rice. Cover and cook on low 3½ hours, or until rice is tender. Check after 3 hours. If liquid is absorbed, but rice is not tender, add 1 more cup water. When rice is tender, stir in shrimp and snow peas. Cook 30 minutes longer. Sprinkle with toasted coconut. Makes 4 servings.

Crawfish and Beans

1 (16-ounce) can pinto beans
1 pound cured ham, diced
1 pound crawfish tails
1 large onion, diced
4 large garlic cloves, minced
1 pound smoked sausage
Hot sauce or red pepper flakes, to taste
¾ cup rice

Place the first 3 ingredients in a slow cooker, and cover with water. Cook on low for 8 to 10 hours. In a pot large enough to hold the beans, sauté the onion, garlic, sausage, and hot sauce or pepper. When the onions are translucent, add beans to pot along with rice, and simmer until rice is tender. Makes 4 servings.

Curried Shrimp

1 pound shrimp, peeled and deveined
2 garlic cloves, minced
2 tablespoons grated fresh ginger
1 onion, chopped
1 red bell pepper, chopped
1½ teaspoons salt
1 teaspoon black pepper
1 tablespoon curry powder
1 (13-ounce) can coconut milk
¼ cup fresh lime juice
Cooked rice
Fresh chopped cilantro

In a slow cooker, combine shrimp, garlic, ginger, onion, bell pepper, salt, pepper, curry powder, coconut milk, and lime juice. Cover and cook on low 4 to 6 hours. Serve over rice, garnished with cilantro. Makes 4 servings.

Fish au Gratin

6 tablespoons butter
3 tablespoons all-purpose flour
1½ teaspoons salt
1 teaspoon black pepper
1½ cups milk
1 tablespoon lemon juice
1 cup grated Parmesan cheese
3 pounds white fish fillets
2 tablespoons chopped green onion

In a skillet, melt butter over medium heat. Add flour, salt, and pepper; stir. Slowly add milk, stirring constantly until thickened. Add lemon juice and cheese. Put fish fillets into a slow cooker. Pour sauce over fish. Cover and cook on high for 1 to 2 hours, or until fish is cooked through. Serve garnished with green onion. Makes 8 servings.

Greek Shrimp

1 medium onion, chopped
1 garlic clove, minced
2 tablespoons olive oil
1 (28-ounce) can diced tomatoes
1 (12-ounce) can tomato paste
¼ cup water
2 tablespoons chopped fresh parsley
1 teaspoon dried oregano
¼ teaspoon black pepper
1½ pounds medium shrimp, peeled and deveined
2 ounces crumbled feta cheese

Sauté the onion and garlic in the olive oil, about 4 to 5 minutes, or until onion is soft. Combine all ingredients except shrimp and feta in slow cooker. Cover and cook on low for 6 to 8 hours. Turn heat to high; add shrimp and cook about 15 minutes or until just pink. Stir in feta cheese. Makes 6 servings.

Poached Salmon

1 pound salmon fillets
½ cup sliced onion
2 fresh thyme sprigs
1 bay leaf
½ teaspoon salt
¼ teaspoon black pepper
¾ cup water
¼ cup chicken broth
1 tablespoon fresh lemon juice

Place the salmon fillets in the bottom of a slow cooker. Top with remaining ingredients. Cover and cook on low for 2 to 3 hours, or until salmon flakes easily with a fork. Makes 4 servings.

Salmon Chowder

3 ounces onions, chopped
6 ounces celery, chopped
4 to 5 ounces shoestring carrots
3 cups fat-free chicken broth
¼ cup brown rice
8 ounces fat-free cream cheese, cubed and softened
12 ounces canned Alaskan salmon, drained and flaked
1 tablespoon fresh dill weed
1 teaspoon salt (optional)
¼ cup water

In slow cooker, combine onion, celery, carrots, chicken broth, and rice. Cover and cook on low for 4 to 5 hours. When vegetables are soft to your preference, turn slow cooker on high, add cream cheese, and stir until melted. Add salmon, spices, and ¼ cup water; stir. Cover and cook about 10 to 20 more minutes on high, stirring occasionally. Makes 4 servings.

Salmon Loaf

1 (16-ounce) can salmon
2 eggs, beaten
1½ cups soft breadcrumbs
¼ cup onion, finely chopped
2 tablespoons butter or margarine
1 tablespoon snipped fresh parsley
1 tablespoon lemon juice
¼ teaspoon salt
Dash cayenne pepper
½ cup shredded sharp Cheddar cheese

Drain salmon; reserve juice. Combine juice with remaining ingredients except the salmon and cheese. Flake salmon; stir into mixture. Shape into round loaf. Line the slow cooker with aluminum foil to come up 2 to 3 inches on sides. Place loaf on foil, not touching sides. Cover and cook on low for 4 to 5 hours. Add the cheese during the last 5 minutes of cooking. Makes 4 servings.

Sausage and Seafood Ragout

1 tablespoon olive oil
1 pound chorizo or mild Italian sausage, cut into chunks
1 onion, diced
2 garlic cloves, minced
½ cup diced celery
½ teaspoon dried thyme
1 small eggplant, cut into 1-inch cubes
1 (28-ounce) can diced tomatoes
¾ cup water or fish stock
¼ cup tomato paste
1 tablespoon sweet paprika
2 pounds mussels
12 ounces catfish or grouper fillets
2 tablespoons chopped fresh parsley

In large skillet, heat oil over medium-high heat; brown sausage, in batches. Transfer to slow cooker. Drain fat from skillet. Add onion, garlic, celery, and thyme; cook, stirring often, until softened, about 5 minutes. Add to slow cooker. Add eggplant, tomatoes, water or stock, tomato paste, and paprika to slow cooker. Cover and cook on low for 6 hours, or until eggplant is tender.

Meanwhile, scrub mussels; trim off any beards. Discard any that do not close when tapped. Cut fish into 2-inch pieces. Add mussels and fish to slow cooker, pushing into liquid. Cover and cook on high until mussels open, about 20 minutes. Discard any that do not open. Sprinkle with parsley. Makes 4 servings.

Scalloped Oysters

1 quart oysters
2 cups saltine cracker crumbs
1½ cups breadcrumbs
⅔ cup grated Parmesan cheese
¾ cup butter, melted
2 eggs, beaten
Salt and black pepper, to taste

In a large bowl, combine all the ingredients, and mix well. Pour into a greased slow cooker. Cover and cook on low for 5 to 6 hours. Makes 4 servings.

Seafood Naples

1 (9-ounce) can shrimp, drain
1 (14-ounce) can tuna, drained
1 (12-ounce) can crab, drained and picked over
4 ounces chopped pimento, drained
⅓ cup chopped fresh parsley
3 cups instant rice
2 (10¾-ounce) cans cream of mushroom soup
3 cups water
1 cup fish stock
1 tablespoon chopped onion
2 teaspoons fresh dill weed
½ teaspoon paprika
½ teaspoon hot pepper sauce

Combine all ingredients in slow cooker. Stir to mix. Cover and cook on low for 3 to 4 hours, until rice is tender. Makes 4 servings.

Seafood Newburg

1 tablespoon butter
½ cup chopped onion
½ cup chopped green bell pepper
2 (10-ounce) cans cream of shrimp soup
1½ cups milk
1 pound shrimp, peeled, deveined, and cooked
1 cup lobster tail meat, cooked and chopped
1½ cups lump crabmeat
1 tablespoon paprika
1 teaspoon salt
½ teaspoon black pepper
Cooked rice

In a skillet, melt the butter over medium heat. Add the onion and bell pepper, and sauté until tender, 2 to 3 minutes. Pour into a slow cooker along with the rest of the ingredients. Cover and cook on low for 4 to 6 hours. Serve with rice. Makes 4 servings.

Shrimp Creole

2 tablespoons butter
1 cup diced celery
1 cup chopped onion
1 cup chopped green bell pepper
1 garlic clove, minced
1 (6-ounce) can tomato paste
1 (28-ounce) can whole tomatoes
1 cup water
1 bay leaf
1 teaspoon salt
¼ teaspoon black pepper
2 teaspoons hot sauce
2 pounds shrimp, peeled and deveined
Cooked rice

In a skillet, melt the butter over medium heat. Sauté celery, onion, bell pepper, and garlic in butter until soft, about 2 to 3 minutes. Pour into a slow cooker along with tomato paste, tomatoes, water, bay leaf, salt, pepper, and hot sauce. Cover and cook on high for 3 to 4 hours. Add shrimp during the last hour of cooking. Serve with rice. Makes 8 servings.

Shrimp Jambalaya

1 pound boneless, skinless chicken thighs, cut into 2-inch pieces
2 stalks celery, thinly sliced
1 medium green bell pepper, cut into 1-inch pieces
1 medium onion, chopped
2 garlic cloves, minced
1 (28-ounce) can crushed tomatoes, with liquid
1 tablespoon white sugar
½ teaspoon salt
½ teaspoon dried Italian seasoning
¼ teaspoon cayenne pepper
1 bay leaf
1 cup uncooked orzo pasta
1 pound shrimp, cooked, peeled, and deveined

In a slow cooker, mix chicken, celery, green bell pepper, onion, garlic, tomatoes, sugar, salt, Italian seasoning, cayenne pepper, and bay leaf. Cover and cook on low for 7 to 9 hours. Remove bay leaf from chicken mixture, and stir in orzo. Increase heat to high. Cook for 15 minutes, until orzo is tender. Stir in shrimp, and cook for 2 minutes, until shrimp are heated through. Makes 8 servings.

Shrimp Marinara

1 (28-ounce) can diced tomatoes
1 (6-ounce) can tomato paste
1 onion, finely chopped
1 garlic clove, minced
1 tablespoon chopped fresh basil
1 teaspoon dried oregano
½ teaspoon salt
¼ teaspoon black pepper
½ teaspoon sugar
1 pound shrimp, peeled and deveined
Cooked spaghetti noodles
¼ cup grated Parmesan cheese

In a slow cooker, combine the tomatoes, tomato paste, onion, garlic, basil, oregano, salt, pepper, and sugar. Cover and cook on low for 6 to 7 hours. Add shrimp during the last hour of cooking. Serve over spaghetti, topped with cheese. Makes 4 servings.

Snapper Vera Cruz

1 tablespoon olive oil
1 large onion, finely chopped
2 garlic cloves, minced
½ teaspoon dried oregano
1 teaspoon chopped cilantro
¼ teaspoon sugar
¼ teaspoon ground cumin
2 jalapeños, finely chopped
1 (28-ounce) can diced tomatoes, drained
½ cup fish stock
4 (8- to 10-ounce) snapper fillets, butterflied
Salt and black pepper, to taste
2 tablespoons lemon juice
1 tablespoon capers
1 small jar sliced green olives

In a skillet, heat oil over medium heat. Sauté onion until softened. Add garlic, oregano, cilantro, sugar, cumin, and jalapeños. Sauté until fragrant, about 1 minute. Add the tomatoes and stock, and bring to a boil.

Transfer to a slow cooker. Cover and cook on high for 3 to 4 hours. Season the fish fillets with salt and pepper, and add to slow cooker with lemon juice. Cover and continue cooking until fish is done, about 20 minutes. Stir in capers and green olives. Makes 4 servings.

Swiss Crab Casserole

4 tablespoons butter
¼ cup chopped celery
1 medium onion, chopped
½ green bell pepper, chopped
4 tablespoons all-purpose flour
2½ cups crab or shrimp stock
1 cup instant rice
2 cups crabmeat
2½ cups shredded Swiss cheese, divided
1 cup sliced mushrooms
1 cup breadcrumbs
½ cup shredded Swiss cheese

In a large saucepan, melt the butter over medium heat. Add the celery, onion, and bell pepper, and sauté until tender, about 3 to 5 minutes. Stir in flour and stock, and bring to a boil. Cook until slightly thickened, about 2 minutes. In a slow cooker, combine rice, crabmeat, 2 cups Swiss cheese, and mushrooms. Pour in sauce and stir lightly. Cover and cook on high for 3 to 5 hours. Pour into a casserole, and cover with breadcrumbs. Sprinkle ½ cup Swiss cheese on top, and put under a broiler until cheese melts. Makes 4 servings.

Tuna Casserole

2 (10-ounce) cans cream of chicken soup
1 cup milk
2 (7-ounce) cans tuna, drained
½ cup chopped onion
1 cup frozen peas
1½ cups dried elbow macaroni, cooked according to package directions
1 cup sliced mushrooms

In a small bowl, mix together the soup and milk. Pour into a slow cooker along with the rest of the ingredients. Cover and cook on high for 3 to 4 hours. Makes 4 servings.

DESSERTS

Apple Pie

8 tart apples, peeled, cored, and sliced
1¼ teaspoons ground cinnamon
¼ teaspoon ground allspice
¼ teaspoon ground nutmeg
¾ cup milk
2 tablespoons butter, softened
¾ cup sugar
2 eggs
2 teaspoons vanilla
1½ cups biscuit mix, divided
⅓ cup brown sugar
3 tablespoons butter, cold

Toss apples in a large bowl with cinnamon, allspice, and nutmeg. Place apple mixture in a lightly greased slow cooker. Combine milk, butter, sugar, eggs, vanilla, and ½ cup biscuit mix. Spoon over apples.

Combine the remaining biscuit mix with the brown sugar. Cut cold butter into biscuit mixture until crumbly. Sprinkle this mixture over top of apple mixture. Cover and cook on low 6 to 7 hours, or until apples are soft. Makes 8 servings.

Apple Slump with Dumplings

6 apples, peeled, cored, and sliced
½ cup apple juice
½ cup brown sugar
1 teaspoon ground cinnamon
¼ teaspoon ground nutmeg
Dash salt
1 cup flour
1½ teaspoons baking powder
½ cup sugar
½ teaspoon salt
1 egg, beaten
½ cup milk
½ cup butter, melted
Whipped cream

In a slow cooker, combine apples, juice, brown sugar, cinnamon, nutmeg, and a pinch of salt. Cover and cook on low for 4 hours.

When the apples are almost done, sift together the flour, baking powder, sugar, and salt. In a separate bowl, whisk together the egg, milk, and melted butter. Combine the wet and dry ingredients and mix thoroughly. Drop by tablespoonfuls into the slow cooker. Cover and cook on high for 45 more minutes. Serve topped with whipped cream. Makes 8 servings.

Baked Apples

8 red apples, cored but not peeled
1¼ cups brown sugar
4 tablespoons cinnamon
½ cup raisins
1½ tablespoons orange zest
⅓ cup butter, melted
2½ cups very hot water

In a small buttered pan, place the apples standing up. In a small bowl, mix together the brown sugar, cinnamon, raisins, orange zest, and melted butter. Fill the apples with this mixture. Place the pan in a slow cooker, and pour hot water around it. Cover and cook on low for 3 to 5 hours, or until apples are tender. Makes 8 servings.

Bananas Foster

½ cup butter
½ cup brown sugar
6 bananas, peeled and sliced
½ teaspoon vanilla extract
1 teaspoon ground cinnamon
Vanilla ice cream

Melt butter in a slow cooker over low heat. Slowly mix in brown sugar. Add the bananas, vanilla extract, and cinnamon, and cook on low for 1 hour. Serve over vanilla ice cream. Makes 6 servings.

Bananas in Honey Ginger Syrup

4 ripe bananas, sliced lengthwise and halved
⅔ cup orange juice
1 tablespoon honey
1 piece crystallized ginger, chopped
2 teaspoons shredded unsweetened coconut
½ teaspoon ground cinnamon

Combine all the ingredients in a slow cooker. Cook on low for 3 to 4 hours. Makes 4 servings.

Banana Nut Bread

1½ cups sugar
½ cup butter, softened
2 eggs
4 small ripe bananas, mashed
3 tablespoons water or milk
2 cups all-purpose flour
1 teaspoon baking soda
½ cup chopped pecans

Cream sugar and butter. Beat in eggs one at a time. Add bananas and milk. Thoroughly mix in remaining ingredients. Pour into a greased 2-pound coffee can. Place in a slow cooker. Cook on high for 3 hours. Makes 8 servings.

Blueberry Cobbler

1 (16-ounce) can blueberry pie filling
1¾ cups biscuit mix
1 egg
3 tablespoons evaporated milk
½ teaspoon ground cinnamon

Lightly butter a slow cooker. Place pie filling in prepared slow cooker and cook on high for 30 minutes. Mix together the remaining ingredients in a medium bowl until crumbly and spoon onto the hot pie filling. Cover and cook on low for 2 to 3 hours. Makes 4 servings.

Blueberry Dump Cake

4 cups fresh blueberries
½ cup sugar
1 (18½-ounce) package yellow cake mix
½ cup butter, melted
Vanilla ice cream

In a small bowl, mix together the blueberries and sugar. Pour into a slow cooker. Combine the cake mix and butter, and pour over the blueberries. Cover and cook on low for 2 to 3 hours. Serve with ice cream. Makes 8 servings.

Brownie Pudding

1 (18½-ounce) package chocolate cake mix
1 (1-ounce) package instant chocolate pudding mix
1 pint sour cream
4 eggs
¾ cup vegetable oil
1 cup water
1 cup chocolate chips
1 cup toasted and chopped pecans

Spray slow cooker with nonstick cooking spray. Mix all ingredients and pour into slow cooker. Cook on low for 5 hours. Makes 8 servings.

Caramel Apples

4 large tart apples, cored
½ cup apple juice
½ cup brown sugar
12 red hot candies
4 tablespoons butter or margarine
8 caramels
¼ teaspoon cinnamon
Vanilla ice cream (optional)

Peel about ¾-inch off the top of each apple, and place in a slow cooker. Pour juice over apples. Fill the center of each apple with 2 tablespoons of sugar, 3 candies, 1 tablespoon butter, and 2 caramels. Sprinkle with cinnamon. Cover and cook on low for 4 to 6 hours, or until apples are tender. Serve immediately with vanilla ice cream. Makes 4 servings.

Caramel Rice Pudding

3 cups cooked white rice
½ cup raisins
2 teaspoons vanilla extract
1 (14-ounce) can sweetened condensed milk
1 (12-ounce) can evaporated milk
1 tablespoon sugar
1 teaspoon ground cinnamon

Prepare the inside of a slow cooker with cooking spray. Mix all ingredients except sugar and cinnamon in the cooker. Cover and cook on low for 3 to 4 hours, or until liquid is absorbed. Stir pudding before serving and sprinkle with sugar and cinnamon. Serve warm. Makes 8 servings.

Carrot Cake

1½ cups all-purpose flour
¾ cup sugar
2 large eggs, lightly beaten
¼ cup water
⅓ cup vegetable oil
1 teaspoon baking powder
½ teaspoon baking soda
¾ teaspoon ground cinnamon
¼ teaspoon ground nutmeg
1 cup grated carrots

Combine all ingredients in large mixing bowl. Spread batter in greased slow cooker. Cover and cook on low until firm in middle, about 2 hours. Makes 8 servings.

Cherry Chocolate Dessert

1 (21-ounce) can cherry pie filling
1 (18½-ounce) package chocolate cake mix
½ cup melted butter

Place pie filling in a slow cooker. Combine dry cake mix and butter. Sprinkle over filling. Cover and cook on low for 3 hours. Makes 8 servings.

Cherry Cobbler

2 (21-ounce) cans cherry pie filling
1 (18½-ounce) package yellow cake mix
⅓ cup sugar
½ teaspoon ground cinnamon
¼ cup butter, melted

Pour pie filling into a slow cooker. In a large bowl, mix together the yellow cake mix, sugar, cinnamon, and butter. Pour over pie filling. Cover and cook on low for 3 to 4 hours. Makes 8 servings.

Chocolate Applesauce Cake

1½ cups all-purpose flour
2 teaspoons baking soda
1 teaspoon baking powder
⅛ teaspoon salt
6 tablespoons unsalted butter
1 cup sugar
1 cup unsweetened applesauce
1 teaspoon ground cinnamon
1 teaspoon vanilla extract
3 eggs
¼ pound unsweetened chocolate, melted
⅓ cup buttermilk
¾ cup semisweet chocolate chips
½ cup chopped walnuts
¼ cup powdered sugar

Sift first four ingredients together in a bowl. Set aside. Combine butter and sugar in a mixing bowl. Beat with an electric mixer until fluffy. Add next four ingredients, and mix thoroughly. With mixer running, pour in melted chocolate, and mix thoroughly. Add flour mixture, and mix on low speed until just blended. Slowly beat in buttermilk. Stir in chocolate chips and walnuts.

   Transfer batter to a slow cooker on high heat. Smooth top. Cover and cook on high for 2¼ to 2½ hours, or until a tester comes out clean when inserted into center. Remove lid, turn off cooker, and let cake cool in cooker until just barely warm. Run a sharp knife around inside edges of cooker. Use a large spatula to carefully remove cake in one piece. Sprinkle with powdered sugar before serving. Makes 8 servings.

Chocolate Brownie Pudding Cake

¾ cup water
½ cup brown sugar
2 tablespoons cocoa
2½ cups brownie mix
1 egg
¼ cup peanut butter
1 tablespoon margarine, softened
¼ cup water
¼ to ½ cup milk chocolate chips

Combine ¾ cup water, brown sugar, and cocoa in a saucepan. Bring to a boil. In the meantime, combine the remaining ingredients in a small bowl. Whisk together or mix well with a spoon. Spread the batter evenly in the bottom of a lightly buttered slow cooker. Pour boiling mixture over the batter. Cover and cook on high for 2 hours; turn heat off and let stand for another 30 minutes. Spoon into dessert dishes while warm. Makes 8 servings.

Corn Pudding

1 (8-ounce) package cream cheese, softened
2 eggs, beaten
⅓ cup sugar
2⅓ cups frozen sweet corn
1 (16-ounce) can cream-style corn
1 (8½-ounce) package corn muffin mix
1 cup milk
2 tablespoons margarine or butter, melted
1 teaspoon salt
¼ teaspoon ground nutmeg

Lightly grease slow cooker. In mixing bowl, blend cream cheese, eggs, and sugar. Add remaining ingredients, and mix well. Transfer to slow cooker. Cover and cook on high for 3 to 4 hours. Makes 8 servings.

Hot Caramel Dip

1 (12-ounce) can sweetened condensed milk
1 cup brown sugar
½ cup butter
½ cup light corn syrup
Apple slices

Mix together all ingredients except apples in saucepan. Bring to boil. Pour into slow cooker set on low. Dip apple slices into hot caramel. Makes about 3 cups.

Indian Pudding

1 cup yellow cornmeal
½ cup molasses
¼ cup sugar
¼ cup butter
¼ teaspoon salt
¼ teaspoon baking soda
2 eggs
6 cups hot milk, divided

In a saucepan, combine all ingredients with 3 cups of the milk. Bring to a simmer. Stir in remaining milk, and transfer to a slow cooker. Cover and cook on low for 5 to 7 hours. Makes 8 servings.

Indian Rice Pudding

4 cups milk
¼ cup basmati or jasmine rice
¾ cup sugar
½ teaspoon ground cardamom
Dash ground nutmeg
2 tablespoons slivered blanched almonds
1 teaspoon rosewater (optional)

Mix the milk, rice, sugar, and cardamom in the slow cooker. Cover and cook on low for 6 to 7 hours, until rice is very soft. Remove and stir in nutmeg and almonds. Serve warm or cool. Sprinkle with rosewater before serving. Makes 4 servings.

Lemon Pudding Cake

3 eggs, separated
¼ cup lemon juice
1 tablespoon grated lemon peel
3 tablespoons butter, melted
1½ cups milk
¾ cup sugar
¼ cup all-purpose flour
⅛ teaspoon salt

In a small bowl, beat egg whites until stiff peaks form. In another bowl, beat egg yolks, and slowly stir in lemon juice, butter, and milk. Sift together sugar, flour, and salt; add to egg yolk mixture, beating until smooth. Stir in egg whites, and pour into a slow cooker. Cover and cook on low for 4 to 6 hours. Makes 8 servings.

Pumpkin Chocolate Marble Cheesecake

1½ cups crumbled gingersnap cookies
½ cup finely chopped pecans
3 tablespoons light brown sugar
⅓ cup butter, melted
2 (8-ounce) packages cream cheese, softened
¾ cup sugar
1 teaspoon vanilla
3 eggs
¾ teaspoon ground cinnamon
¼ teaspoon ground nutmeg
1 (15-ounce) can pumpkin pureé
½ cup whipping cream
4 ounces semisweet chocolate, melted
Very hot water

In a large bowl, combine the cookie crumbs, pecans, brown sugar, and melted butter. Mix thoroughly. Press into a greased 7-inch springform pan, and put in the freezer for at least 30 minutes.

In the bowl of an electric mixer, combine cream cheese, sugar, and vanilla. Add eggs one at a time, mixing thoroughly after each addition. While mixer is running, add cinnamon, nutmeg, pumpkin, and whipping cream. Pour batter into the pie shell, and top with melted chocolate. Gently insert a knife or fork into the pie and slowly make circular motions to create the marbling effect. Cover pie with aluminum foil.

Place pie in a slow cooker and pour hot water around it, enough to fill the slow cooker about 1 inch. Cover and cook on high for 3 to 4 hours. Remove from slow cooker and place in refrigerator; chill for at least 2 hours before serving. Makes 8 servings.

Pumpkin Pudding

1 egg
2 egg whites
1¾ cups pumpkin purée
3 cups evaporated skim milk
1 teaspoon margarine
⅓ cup brown sugar
⅓ cup white sugar
1 teaspoon ground cinnamon
½ teaspoon ground allspice
½ teaspoon ground nutmeg
½ cup raisins or chopped dates
2 cups soft breadcrumbs

Beat the egg and egg whites together until they are a light lemon color. Combine the eggs, pumpkin, milk, and margarine in a slow cooker. Stir in remaining ingredients. Cover and cook on low for 5½ to 7½ hours until a knife inserted in the center of the pudding comes out clean. Makes 6 servings.

Rice Pudding

1 cup white rice
1 cup sugar
2 (12-ounce) cans evaporated milk
1 teaspoon vanilla extract
1 teaspoon ground cinnamon
1 teaspoon ground nutmeg

Combine all the ingredients in a slow cooker. Cover and cook on low for 1½ hours, stirring occasionally, until rice is tender. Makes 4 servings.

Slow Cooker Candy

1 (16-ounce) package dry-roasted salted peanuts
1 (16-ounce) package dry-roasted unsalted peanuts
1 (12-ounce) package semisweet chocolate bits
1 bar German chocolate
32 barks white almond

Add peanuts to the bottom of the slow cooker. Pour in the other ingredients. Cook on low for 1 to 2 hours. Lay out wax paper on the counter. Drop candy by spoonfuls on the wax paper, and let cool. Makes 16 servings.

Streusel Cake

1 (16-ounce) package pound cake mix
¼ cup brown sugar
1 tablespoon all-purpose flour
¼ cup finely chopped nuts
1 teaspoon ground cinnamon

Mix cake batter according to directions on package. Liberally grease and flour a 2-pound coffee tin. Pour cake batter into the coffee tin. Mix brown sugar, flour, nuts, and cinnamon together. Sprinkle over top of cake mix. Place coffee tin in slow cooker. Cover with several layers of paper towels. Cover and cook on high for 3 to 4 hours. Makes 8 servings.

Triple Chocolate Mess

1 (18½-ounce) package chocolate cake mix
2 cups sour cream
1 (1-ounce) package instant chocolate pudding
1 (8-ounce) package semisweet chocolate chips
¾ cup vegetable oil
4 eggs
1 cup water

Coat inside of a slow cooker with cooking spray. In a large bowl, combine all the ingredients, and mix thoroughly. Pour the batter into the slow cooker. Cover and cook on low for 5 to 6 hours. Makes 12 servings.

BEVERAGES

Apple Cider

2 (4-inch) sticks cinnamon, broken into small pieces
1 teaspoon whole cloves
1 teaspoon whole allspice
2 quarts apple cider
½ cup packed brown sugar
1 medium orange, sliced

Place cinnamon, cloves, and allspice in a double thickness of cheesecloth; bring up the corners of cloth, and tie with a string to form a bag. Place cider and brown sugar in a slow cooker; stir until sugar dissolves. Add spice bag. Place orange slices on top. Cover and cook on low for 2 to 5 hours. Remove spice bag before serving. Makes 8 servings.

Apple Cider with Mango and Orange

¾ gallon apple cider
4 orange tea bags
4 mango tea bags
2 cinnamon sticks
½ cup brown sugar
1 orange

Add apple cider, tea bags, cinnamon, and brown sugar to slow cooker. Cut orange into slices, and add to slow cooker. Cook on high for 1 hour. Turn to low for serving. Makes 20 servings.

Cranberry Punch

2 cups cranberry juice
2 quarts apple cider
½ cup sugar
1 orange studded with 6 whole cloves
2 cinnamon sticks (3 inches each)
Orange slices or cinnamon sticks, for garnishes

Combine all ingredients except garnish in slow cooker. Simmer covered on low for 1½ hours. Serve in warmed mugs. Garnish each with orange slice or cinnamon stick. Makes 6 servings.

Hot Buttered Punch

¾ cup brown sugar
4 cups water
¼ teaspoon salt
¼ teaspoon ground nutmeg
½ teaspoon ground cinnamon
½ teaspoon ground allspice
¾ teaspoon ground cloves
2 (16-ounce) cans jellied cranberry sauce
1 quart pineapple juice
Cinnamon sticks
Butter

In slow cooker, combine brown sugar with water, salt, nutmeg, cinnamon, allspice, and cloves. Break up cranberry sauce with fork. Add cranberry sauce and pineapple juice to slow cooker. Cover and heat on low for 3 to 4 hours. Serve hot in mugs with cinnamon sticks. Dot each with a pat of butter. Makes 6 to 8 servings.

Pomegranate Punch

3 cups pomegranate juice
1 cup cranberry juice
½ cup orange juice
1 cinnamon stick
1 tablespoon grated fresh ginger, or 1 teaspoon ground ginger
Orange zest

Combine all ingredients except zest in slow cooker, and stir well to combine. Cover and cook on low for 2 to 3 hours until hot. Garnish cups with orange zest. Makes 4 servings.

Spicy Tomato Sipper

1 (46-ounce) can vegetable juice
1 stalk celery, halved crosswise
2 tablespoons brown sugar
2 tablespoons lemon juice
1½ teaspoons prepared horseradish
1 teaspoon Worcestershire sauce
½ teaspoon hot sauce

In a slow cooker, combine all ingredients. Cover and cook on low heat for 4 to 6 hours or on high for 1½ to 2 hours. Discard celery. Ladle beverage into cups. Makes 4 to 6 servings.

Viennese Coffee

3 cups strong freshly brewed hot coffee
3 tablespoons chocolate syrup
1 teaspoon sugar
⅓ cup heavy cream
Whipped cream
Chocolate shavings

Combine coffee, chocolate syrup, and sugar in a slow cooker. Cover and cook on low for 2 to 2½ hours. Stir in heavy cream. Cover and cook 30 minutes or until heated through. Ladle coffee into coffee cups. Top with whipped cream and chocolate shavings. Makes 3 servings.

White Hot Cocoa

2 cups heavy whipping cream
6 cups milk
12 ounces white chocolate
1 teaspoon vanilla extract

Place ingredients in a slow cooker, and heat on low 2 to 2½ hours, or until chocolate is melted and mixture is hot; stir well to blend. Makes 10 servings.

365 Easy Slow Cooker Recipes Index

A

Acapulco Flank Steak 114
Adobo Chicken 156
All-Day-Long Beef 114
Almond Chicken 156
Aloha Chicken 157

Appetizers
   Appetizer Ribs 10
   Bacon Horseradish Dip 10
   Bacon Onion Dip 11
   Beef Dip 11
   Boiled Peanuts 12
   Cajun Pecans 12
   Cheddar Potato Slices 13
   Cheesy Chile and Refried
     Bean Dip 13
   Cheesy New Orleans Shrimp
     Dip 14
   Chili con Queso 14
   Chili Dip 15
   Chili Nuts 15
   Cocktail Sausages....................16
   Crab Dip 16
   Cranberry Turkey Balls 17
   Enchilada Dip 18
   Hearty Broccoli Dip 18
   Hot Spinach Cheese Dip 19
   Kielbasa Sausage 19
   Marinara Dip 20
   Marinated Mushrooms 20
   Party Snack Mix 21
   Reuben Spread 21
   Roasted Pepper and Artichoke
     Spread....................................22
   Salsa 22
   Seafood Fondue 23
   Sloppy Joe Dip 23
   Spicy Beef Dip 24
   Spicy Chicken Wings 24
   Spinach and Artichoke Dip 25
   Stuffed Chicken Rolls 25
   Sweet and Sour Meatballs 26
   Turkey and Cheese Dip 26

Appetizer Ribs 10
Apple Cider 240
Apple Cider with Mango and
   Orange 240
Apple Pie 222
Apple Slump with Dumplings....223
Appley Kielbasa 115
Asian-Spiced Chicken and
   Beans 157

B

Baby Back Ribs 115
Bacon Horseradish Dip 10
Bacon Onion Dip..........................11
Baked Apples 224
Baked Beans 28
Baked Salmon 204
Banana Nut Bread 225
Bananas Foster.........................224
Bananas in Honey Ginger
   Syrup......................................225
Barbecue Sandwich 116
Barbecue Turkey Sandwich.....158
Barbecued Bean Soup 47
Barbecued Pinto Beans 28
Beach Boy Pot Roast................116
Bean and Bacon Soup 47
Bean Soup 48

Beef
   6-Can Chili 46
   8-Can Soup 46
   Acapulco Flank Steak 114

244 • Index

365 Easy Slow Cooker Recipes Index

All-Day-Long Beef 114
Barbecue Sandwich 116
Beach Boy Pot Roast 116
Beef and Black-Eyed Peas 117
Beef and Broccoli....................117
Beef and Potatoes...................118
Beef Broccoli Soup 48
Beef Dip 11
Beef Stew 49
Beef Taco Bean Soup 50
Best Bean Chili 50
Buffalo Stew with Shiitake
 Mushrooms 56
Cajun Beef and Potatoes 118
Camper's Stew 56
Caribbean Ribs 119
Cheeseburgers........................120
Chili Beef Sandwiches 121
Chili Dip....................................15
Chuck Roast au Gratin 121
Corned Beef and Cabbage 122
Cowboy Stew 67
Curried Beef 125
Dinner Party Stew 70
Dutch Chili Soup 71
Firehouse Chili 72
Firehouse Stew 73
Forgotten Minestrone 75
French Dip Sandwich..............126
French Onion Beef 126
Greek Chili 78
Hamburger Stew 81
Hearty Broccoli Dip 18
Hungarian Goulash.................129
Hungry Man 130
Italian Roast Beef...................131
Italian Wedding Soup 82
Meatball Soup 84
Meatballs 135

Meatloaf 136
Mexican Beef Soup 84
Mexican Ribs 137
Mushroom-Smothered Beef 137
Old-Fashioned Pot Roast 138
Onion Meatballs 138
Prima Donna Chili 91
Reuben Spread 21
Roman Stew 93
Roulade Steak........................145
Saucy Beef 146
Savory Short Ribs...................146
Sloppy Joes............................147
Smoky Barbecue Brisket 148
Southwestern Beef Soup 97
Spiced Beef Brisket 149
Spicy Beef Dip 24
Sweet and Sour Meatballs 26
Tamale Pie 150
Tangy Rump Roast 151
Tender Shredded Beef 152
Teriyaki Steak.........................152
Tex-Mex Beef Stew 99
Thick and Spicy Chili...............101
Vegetable and Beef Soup 106
Viennese Pot Roast................153
Beef and Black-Eyed Peas 117
Beef and Broccoli 117
Beef and Potatoes 118
Beef Broccoli Soup 48
Beef Dip 11
Beef Stew 49
Beef Taco Bean Soup 50
Best Bean Chili 50

Beverages
Apple Cider .....:....................240
Apple Cider with Mango and
 Orange 240
Cranberry Punch....................241

Index • 245

365 Easy Slow Cooker Recipes Index

Beverages cont.
Hot Buttered Punch 241
Pomegranate Punch 242
Spicy Tomato Sipper 242
Viennese Coffee 243
White Hot Cocoa 243
Black Bean Chili 51
Black Bean Mushroom Stew 53
Black Bean Soup with Chipotle
  Chiles 52
Black Bean Soup with Crab 51
Black-Eyed Pea Soup 54
Blueberry Cobbler 226
Blueberry Dump Cake 226
Boiled Peanuts 12
Bouillabaisse 204
Brown Rice and Mushroom
  Soup 54
Brown Sugar Chicken 158
Brownie Pudding 227
Brunswick Stew 55
Buffalo Chicken Wing Soup 55
Buffalo Stew with Shiitake
  Mushrooms 56

C

Cajun Beef and Potatoes 118
Cajun Pecans 12
Camper's Stew 56
Canadian Bacon Soup 57
Cantonese Pork 119
Caramel Apples 227
Caramel Rice Pudding 228
Caramelized Onions 29
Caribbean Ribs 119
Caribbean Shrimp 205
Caribbean Shrimp and Rice........205

Carrot Cake 228
Cauliflower Soup 57
Cheddar Potato Slices 13

Cheese
Cheddar Potato Slices 13
Cheeseburger Chowder.............58
Cheeseburgers..........................120
Cheesy Asparagus 29
Cheesy Broccoli and
  Cauliflower 30
Cheesy Chicken 159
Cheesy Chile and Refried Bean
  Dip 13
Cheesy New Orleans Shrimp
  Dip 14
Cheesy Potatoes 30
Cheesy Sausage and
  Tortellini 120
Cheesy Spinach 31
Chili con Queso 14
Hot Spinach Cheese Dip 19
Macaroni and Cheese 37
Potato Cheese Soup 89
Spinach and Artichoke Dip 25
Turkey and Cheese Dip 26
Cheeseburger Chowder 58
Cheeseburgers 120
Cheesy Asparagus 29
Cheesy Broccoli and
  Cauliflower 30
Cheesy Chicken 159
Cheesy Chile and Refried Bean
  Dip 13
Cheesy New Orleans Shrimp
  Dip 14
Cheesy Potatoes 30
Cheesy Sausage and Tortellini..120
Cheesy Spinach 31
Cherry Chocolate Dessert 229

365 Easy Slow Cooker Recipes Index

Cherry Cobbler 229
Chicken and Dumplings 159
Chicken and Rice Soup 58
Chicken and Shrimp 160
Chicken and Shrimp
    Jambalaya 161
Chicken Artichoke Casserole......161
Chicken Casserole 162
Chicken Chili..................................59
Chicken Chowder 59
Chicken Cordon Bleu 162
Chicken Dinner 163
Chicken Divan 163
Chicken Marengo 164
Chicken Noodle Soup 60
Chicken Soup.................................61
Chicken Spaghetti 164
Chicken Stew.................................62
Chicken Stew with Pepper and
    Pineapple...............................63
Chicken Stroganoff 165
Chicken Tacos 165
Chicken Taco Soup 64
Chicken Tortillas 166
Chicken Wings.............................166
Chicken with Mushrooms and
    Basil 167
Chili Beef Sandwiches 121
Chili con Queso.............................14
Chili Dip 15
Chili Nuts.......................................15
Chinese Turkey Stew 65

Chocolate
    Brownie Pudding 227
    Cherry Chocolate Dessert 229
    Chocolate Applesauce Cake 230
    Chocolate Brownie Pudding
        Cake 231
    Pumpkin Chocolate Marble

Cheesecake 234
Slow Cooker Candy 236
Triple Chocolate Mess 237
Viennese Coffee 243
White Hot Cocoa 243
Chocolate Applesauce Cake 230
Chocolate Brownie Pudding
    Cake 231
Chow Mein Casserole 206
Chuck Roast au Gratin 121
Chutney Ham..............................122
Chunky Pizza Soup 66
Cinnamon Applesauce 31
Citrus Chicken 168
Cocktail Sausages 16
Coconut Thai Shrimp and Rice ..207
Cola Chicken 168
Collard Greens in Tomato Sauce..32
Corn Pudding..............................231
Corned Beef and Cabbage..........122
Cottage Stew 66
Country Chicken Stew..................67
Cowboy Stew 67
Crab Dip 16
Crab Stew......................................68
Cranberry Pork Roast 123
Cranberry Punch 241
Cranberry Turkey Balls 17
Crawfish and Beans 208
Cream of Mushroom Soup 68
Creamy Asparagus Soup 69
Creamy Chicken 169
Creamy Chicken Casserole 169
Creamy Ham and Potatoes 124
Creamy Italian Chicken..............170
Curried Beef 125
Curried Chicken..........................170
Curried Shrimp 208
Curry Cauliflower Soup................70

Index • 247

D

Desserts
- Apple Pie 222
- Apple Slump with Dumplings 223
- Baked Apples 224
- Banana Nut Bread 225
- Bananas Foster 224
- Bananas in Honey Ginger Syrup 225
- Blueberry Cobbler 226
- Blueberry Dump Cake 226
- Brownie Pudding 227
- Caramel Apples 227
- Caramel Rice Pudding 228

Carrot Cake 228
- Cherry Chocolate Dessert 229
- Cherry Cobbler 229
- Chocolate Applesauce Cake 230
- Chocolate Brownie Pudding Cake 231
- Corn Pudding 231
- Hot Caramel Dip 232
- Indian Pudding 232
- Indian Rice Pudding 233
- Lemon Pudding Cake 233
- Pumpkin Chocolate Marble Cheesecake 234
- Pumpkin Pudding 235
- Rice Pudding 235
- Slow Cooker Candy 236
- Streusel Cake 236
- Triple Chocolate Mess 237

Dinner Party Stew 70
Double Corn Stew 71
Dutch Chili Soup 71
Dutch Country Soup 72

E

Easiest Pork Chops 125
8-Can Soup 46
Enchilada Dip 18

F

Firehouse Chili 72
Firehouse Stew 73
Fish au Gratin 209
Fish Chowder 74
Forgotten Minestrone 75
French Dip Sandwich 126
French Onion Beef 126
French Onion Soup 76
French Turkey 171
Fresh Asparagus Soup 76
Fresh Tomato Soup 77
Fresh Veggie Lasagna 33
Fruit Soup 77

G

Garden Gate Soup 78
Garlic Pepper Chicken 171
Garlic Roasted Chicken with Butter 172
Gingered Carrots 34
Glazed Carrots 34
Greek Chili 78
Greek Shrimp 209
Greek Stew 79
Gumbo 80

365 Easy Slow Cooker Recipes Index

H

Ham and Beans 127
Ham and Lentil Stew 80
Ham and Scalloped Potatoes 128
Ham Balls 127
Hamburger Stew 81
Harvest Potatoes 35
Hearty Broccoli Dip 18
Herbed Turkey Cutlets 173
Home-Style Baked Beans 35
Home-Style Turkey Dinner 174
Honey Barbecue Pork and
    Carrots 128
Honey Hoisin Chicken 175
Honey Mustard Pork Roast 129
Hot Buttered Punch 241
Hot Caramel Dip 232
Hot Dog Beans 36
Hot German Potato Salad 36
Hot Spinach Cheese Dip 19
Hungarian Goulash 129
Hungry Man 130
Hunter's Turkey 176

I

Indian Pudding 232
Indian Rice Pudding 233
Irish Stew 83
Island Chicken 177
Island Ribs 130
Italian Chicken 177
Italian Pork Chops 131
Italian Roast Beef 131
Italian Sausage Soup 81
Italian Turkey Sandwiches 178
Italian Wedding Soup 82

J

Jamaican Chicken Curry 179

K

Kielbasa Sausage 19
Kielbasa Stew 83
Kona Chicken 179

L

Lamb
    Lamb and Veggie Curry 132
    Lamb Chops with Tomatoes 133
    Lamb Shanks 133
    Marinated Lamb 134
Lamb and Veggie Curry 132
Lamb Chops with Tomatoes 133
Lamb Shanks 133
Lacquered Chicken 180
Lemon Chicken 180
Lemon Pepper Chicken 181
Lemon Pudding Cake 233
Lightened Mashed Potatoes 37
Lime Chicken 181

M

Macaroni and Cheese 37
Magnificent Mushrooms 38
Maple-Glazed Turkey Breast ... 182
Marinara Dip 20
Marinated Lamb 134
Marinated Mushrooms 20
Mashed Potatoes 38

365 Easy Slow Cooker Recipes Index

Meatball Soup 84
Meatballs 135
Meatloaf..136
Mexican Beef Soup 84
Mexican Chicken Soup 85
Mexican Pork.................................136
Mexican Ribs.................................137
Mexican Turkey.............................183
Mixed Rice Pilaf 39
Moroccan Lentil Stew 86
Moroccan Soup 87
Mushroom-Smothered Beef 137

O

Old-Fashioned Pot Roast............138
Onion and Mushroom Chicken ..184
Onion Meatballs 138
Orange Chicken 184
Orange-Glazed Chicken 185

P

Party Snack Mix 21
Peachy Chicken 185
Peachy Sweet Potatoes 39
Peanut Chicken 186
Pineapple Bean Pot 139
Pineapple Ginger Pork................140
Pizza Chicken 186
Pizza Fondue 141
Poached Salmon 210
Polish Sauerkraut and Apples 141
Polynesian Spareribs 142
Pomegranate Punch 242
Pork
   Appetizer Ribs 10

Appley Kielbasa 115
Baby Back Ribs 115
Bacon Horseradish Dip 10
Bacon Onion Dip 11
Cantonese Pork..........................119
Cheesy Sausage and
   Tortellini 120
Chutney Ham 122
Cocktail Sausages......................16
Cranberry Pork Roast................123
Cranberry Turkey Balls 17
Creamy Ham and Potatoes......124
Easiest Pork Chops....................125
Ham and Beans 127
Ham and Lentil Stew 80
Ham and Scalloped Potatoes ..128
Ham Balls 127
Honey Barbecue Pork and
   Carrots......................................128
Honey Mustard Pork Roast 129
Island Ribs 130
Italian Pork Chops 131
Italian Sausage Soup 81
Mexican Pork 136
Pineapple Bean Pot 139
Pineapple Ginger Pork 140
Pizza Fondue 141
Polish Sauerkraut and Apples..141
Polynesian Spareribs 142
Pork and Black Bean Stew.......88
Pork Chops and Applesauce....142
Pork Fajitas.................................143
Pork in a Bun 144
Pork with Fruit 144
Red Beans and Rice 145
Smoked Sausage and
   Potatoes...................................148
Sweet and Spicy Kielbasa
   Sausage 149

365 Easy Slow Cooker Recipes Index

Sweet Barbecue Ribs 150
Tender Pork Roast 151
Wild Rice Soup 110
Pork and Black Bean Stew 88
Pork Chops and Applesauce 142
Pork Fajitas 143
Pork in a Bun............................144
Pork with Fruit..........................144
Potato Cheese Soup 89
Potato Chowder 90
Potato Soup 90

Poultry

Adobo Chicken......................156
Almond Chicken....................156
Aloha Chicken 157
Asian-Spiced Chicken and
  Beans.................................157
Barbecue Turkey Sandwich 158
Brown Sugar Chicken 158
Brunswick Stew 55
Buffalo Chicken Wing Soup......55
Cheesy Chicken 159
Chicken and Dumplings..........159
Chicken and Rice Soup 58
Chicken and Shrimp................160
Chicken and Shrimp
  Jambalaya 161
Chicken Artichoke Casserole ..161
Chicken Casserole 162
Chicken Chili 59
Chicken Chowder.....................59
Chicken Cordon Bleu 162
Chicken Dinner......................163
Chicken Divan 163
Chicken Marengo 164
Chicken Noodle Soup...............60
Chicken Soup 61
Chicken Spaghetti..................164
Chicken Stew 62

Chicken Stew with Pepper and
  Pineapple.............................63
Chicken Stroganoff................165
Chicken Taco Soup..................64
Chicken Tacos 165
Chicken Tortillas 166
Chicken Wings 166
Chicken with Mushrooms and
  Basil 167
Chinese Turkey Stew 65
Citrus Chicken 168
Cola Chicken 168
Country Chicken Stew 67
Creamy Chicken 169
Creamy Chicken Casserole 169
Creamy Italian Chicken 170
Curried Chicken 170
Enchilada Dip...........................18
French Turkey........................171
Garlic Pepper Chicken 171
Garlic Roasted Chicken with
  Butter 172
Herbed Turkey Cutlets 173
Home-Style Turkey Dinner 174
Honey Hoisin Chicken 175
Hunter's Turkey 176
Island Chicken 177
Italian Chicken 177
Italian Turkey Sandwiches 178
Jamaican Chicken Curry 179
Kielbasa Sausage 19
Kona Chicken........................179
Lacquered Chicken.................180
Lemon Chicken 180
Lemon Pepper Chicken 181
Lime Chicken 181
Maple-Glazed Turkey Breast ..182
Mexican Chicken Soup 85
Mexican Turkey 183

Index • 251

365 Easy Slow Cooker Recipes Index

Poultry cont.
Moroccan Soup 87
Onion and Mushroom
 Chicken 184
Orange Chicken 184
Orange-Glazed Chicken 185
Peachy Chicken 185
Peanut Chicken......................186
Pizza Chicken 186
Pulled Chicken 187
Roasted Chicken....................187
Rustic Stew.............................94
Smothered Chicken and
 Vegetables 188
Sour Cream and Bacon
 Chicken 188
South of the Border Chicken ..189
Southwest Turkey Loaf 189
Soy Chicken 190
Spicy Chicken........................191
Spicy Chicken Wings 24
Split Pea Soup 98
Stuffed Chicken Rolls 25
Sunshine Chicken...................191
Sweet and Sour Chicken 192
Sweet and Sour Chicken Stew ..98
Tangy Chicken Thighs 193
Taverna Chicken 194
Tennessee Chicken Breasts 194
Three-Ingredient Turkey..........195
Turkey and Cheese Dip 26
Turkey Breast 195
Turkey Breast with Marmalade
 Sauce..................................196
Turkey Chili and Beans 102
Turkey Dijon..........................196
Turkey Nachos 197
Turkey Parmesan Meatballs 198
Turkey Roast with

Vegetables 199
Turkey Sandwiches.................200
Turkey Stuffing.......................200
Turkey Teriyaki Sandwich 201
Turkey Tortilla Soup................103
White Chicken Chili................109
White Turkey Chili..................110
Wild Duck 201
Wild Rice-Stuffed Turkey 202
Prima Donna Chili...................91
Prospector's Stew....................91
Pulled Chicken.......................187
Pumpkin Chocolate Marble
 Cheesecake 234
Pumpkin Pudding 235
Pumpkin Soup 92

R

Ravioli Stew............................92
Red Beans and Rice................145
Reuben Spread........................21
Rice Pilaf 40
Rice Pudding 235
Roasted Chicken 187
Roasted Pepper and Artichoke
 Spread 22
Roman Stew............................93
Roulade Steak 145
Rustic Stew 94

S

Salmon Chowder 210
Salmon Loaf 211
Salsa.......................................22
Salt-Baked Potatoes.................40

365 Easy Slow Cooker Recipes Index

Saucy Beef 146
Sausage and Seafood Ragout 212
Savory Short Ribs 146
Savory Tomato Beef Stew 94
Scalloped Oysters 213

Seafood
   Baked Salmon..........................204
   Bouillabaisse 204
   Caribbean Shrimp....................205
   Caribbean Shrimp and Rice 205
   Chow Mein Casserole 206
   Coconut Thai Shrimp and
      Rice 207
   Crab Dip 16
   Crab Stew 68
   Crawfish and Beans 208
   Curried Shrimp........................208
   Fish au Gratin 209
   Fish Chowder 74
   Greek Shrimp 209
   Poached Salmon 210
   Salmon Chowder 210
   Salmon Loaf 211
   Sausage and Seafood Ragout ..212
   Scalloped Oysters....................213
   Seafood Fondue 23
   Seafood Naples.......................213
   Seafood Newburg 214
   Shrimp Creole 215
   Shrimp Jambalaya 216
   Shrimp Marinara 217
   Snapper Vera Cruz 218
   Swiss Crab Casserole 219
   Tuna Casserole 220

Seafood Chowder.........................95
Seafood Fondue 23
Seafood Naples 213
Seafood Newburg 214
Shrimp Creole 215
Shrimp Jambalaya 216
Shrimp Marinara 217
Shrimp Stew..............................96
6-Can Chili 46
Sloppy Joe Dip 23
Sloppy Joes 147
Slow Cooker Candy..................236
Smoked Sausage and Potatoes ..148
Smoky Barbecue Brisket 148
Smothered Chicken and
   Vegetables 188
Snapper Vera Cruz 218

Soups and Stews
6-Can Chili 46
8-Can Soup 46
Barbecued Bean Soup 47
Bean and Bacon Soup 47
Bean Soup 48
Beef Broccoli Soup 48
Beef Stew 49
Beef Taco Bean Soup 50
Best Bean Chili 50
Black Bean Chili 51
Black Bean Mushroom Stew 53
Black Bean Soup with Chipotle
   Chiles 52
Black Bean Soup with Crab 51
Black-Eyed Pea Soup 54
Brown Rice and Mushroom
   Soup 54
Brunswick Stew 55
Buffalo Chicken Wing Soup......55
Buffalo Stew with Shiitake
   Mushrooms 56
Camper's Stew 56
Canadian Bacon Soup 57
Cauliflower Soup 57
Cheeseburger Chowder............58
Chicken and Rice Soup 58

365 Easy Slow Cooker Recipes Index

Soups and Stews cont.

Chicken Chili 59
Chicken Chowder 59
Chicken Noodle Soup 60
Chicken Soup 61
Chicken Stew 62
Chicken Stew with Pepper and
  Pineapple 63
Chicken Taco Soup 64
Chinese Turkey Stew 65
Chunky Pizza Soup 66
Cottage Stew 66
Country Chicken Stew 67
Cowboy Stew 67
Crab Stew 68
Cream of Mushroom Soup 68
Creamy Asparagus Soup 69
Curry Cauliflower Soup 70
Dinner Party Stew 70
Double Corn Stew 71
Dutch Chili Soup 71
Dutch Country Soup 72
Firehouse Chili 72
Firehouse Stew 73
Fish Chowder 74
Forgotten Minestrone 75
French Onion Soup 76
Fresh Asparagus Soup 76
Fresh Tomato Soup 77
Fruit Soup 77
Garden Gate Soup 78
Greek Chili 78
Greek Stew 79
Gumbo 80
Ham and Lentil Stew 80
Hamburger Stew 81
Irish Stew 83
Italian Sausage Soup 81
Italian Wedding Soup 82

Kielbasa Stew 83
Meatball Soup 84
Mexican Beef Soup 84
Mexican Chicken Soup 85
Moroccan Lentil Stew 86
Moroccan Soup 87
Pork and Black Bean Stew 88
Potato Cheese Soup 89
Potato Chowder 90
Potato Soup 90
Prima Donna Chili 91
Prospector's Stew 91
Pumpkin Soup 92
Ravioli Stew 92
Roman Stew 93
Rustic Stew 94
Savory Tomato Beef Stew 94
Seafood Chowder 95
Shrimp Stew 96
Southwestern Beef Soup 97
Spinach, Chicken, and Wild Rice
  Soup 97
Split Pea Soup 98
Sweet and Sour Chicken Stew 98
Tex-Mex Beef Stew 99
Thai Curry Seafood Stew 100
Thick and Spicy Chili 101
Turkey Chili and Beans 102
Turkey Tortilla Soup 103
Tuscan Sausage and Bean
  Soup 104
Vegetable and Barley Soup 105
Vegetable and Beef Soup 106
Vegetable Minestrone 107
Vegetarian Chili 108
White Chicken Chili 109
White Turkey Chili 110
Wild Rice Soup 110
Yellow Pea Chowder 111

365 Easy Slow Cooker Recipes Index

Zucchini and Potato Soup 111
Sour Cream and Bacon
    Chicken...................................188
South of the Border Chicken......189
Southern Potatoes 41
Southwest Turkey Loaf 189
Southwestern Beef Soup 97
Soy Chicken................................190
Spaghetti Squash Frittatas 41
Spiced Beef Brisket....................149
Spicy Beef Dip 24
Spicy Chicken 191
Spicy Chicken Wings...................24
Spicy Tomato Sipper 242
Spinach and Artichoke Dip 25
Spinach, Chicken, and Wild Rice
    Soup 97
Split Pea Soup 98
Streusel Cake 236
Stuffed Chicken Rolls 25
Sunshine Chicken 191
Sweet-and-Sour Chicken 192
Sweet and Sour Chicken Stew......98
Sweet and Sour Meatballs............26
Sweet and Spicy Kielbasa
    Sausage 149
Sweet Barbecue Ribs..................150
Swiss Crab Casserole 219

T

Tamale Pie 150
Tangy Chicken Thighs...............193
Tangy Rump Roast 151
Taverna Chicken 194
Tender Pork Roast 151
Tender Shredded Beef 152
Tennessee Chicken Breasts 194

Teriyaki Steak 152
Tex-Mex Beef Stew 99
Thai Curry Seafood Stew 100
Thick and Spicy Chili 101
Three-Ingredient Turkey 195
Triple Chocolate Mess................237
Tuna Casserole...........................220
Turkey and Cheese Dip 26
Turkey Breast.............................195
Turkey Breast with Marmalade
    Sauce....................................196
Turkey Chili and Beans 102
Turkey Dijon 196
Turkey Nachos...........................197
Turkey Parmesan Meatballs........198
Turkey Roast with Vegetables 199
Turkey Sandwiches 200
Turkey Stuffing 200
Turkey Teriyaki Sandwich..........201
Turkey Tortilla Soup 103
Tuscan Sausage and Bean
    Soup 104

V

Vegetable and Barley Soup 105
Vegetable and Beef Soup............106
Vegetable Minestrone 107
Vegetables and Side Dishes
    Baked Beans............................28
    Barbecued Pinto Beans 28
    Caramelized Onions.................29
    Cheesy Asparagus 29
    Cheesy Broccoli and
        Cauliflower 30
    Cheesy Potatoes 30
    Cheesy Spinach 31
    Cinnamon Applesauce 31

365 Easy Slow Cooker Recipes Index

Vegetables and Side Dishes cont.
Collard Greens in Tomato
  Sauce 32
Fresh Veggie Lasagna................33
Gingered Carrots 34
Glazed Carrots 34
Harvest Potatoes 35
Home-Style Baked Beans..........35
Hot Dog Beans 36
Hot German Potato Salad..........36
Lightened Mashed Potatoes 37
Macaroni and Cheese 37
Magnificent Mushrooms 38
Mashed Potatoes.......................38
Mixed Rice Pilaf........................39
Peachy Sweet Potatoes 39
Rice Pilaf 40
Salt-Baked Potatoes 40
Southern Potatoes.....................41
Spaghetti Squash Frittatas 41
Vegetarian Enchilada
  Casserole..................................42
Vegetarian Stuffed Peppers 43
Wild Rice 44
Vegetarian Chili 108
Vegetarian Enchilada Casserole....42
Vegetarian Stuffed Peppers 43
Viennese Coffee...........................243
Viennese Pot Roast 153

W

White Chicken Chili 109
White Hot Cocoa.........................243
White Turkey Chili 110
Wild Duck 201
Wild Rice.....................................44

Wild Rice Soup 110
Wild Rice-Stuffed Turkey 202

Y

Yellow Pea Chowder 111

Z

Zucchini and Potato Soup 111